Racism, Sexism, and the University
The Political Science Affair at the University of British Columbia

In 1995 a report was released charging faculty members of the Department of Political Science at the University of British Columbia with sexism and racism. The president of UBC responded to the controversial McEwen Report by suspending admissions to the graduate program in political science, sparking a fiery dispute among students and faculty members over the fairness of the decision.

The debate was about sexism and racism, academic freedom, and due process. But it also raised fundamental questions about the nature and purpose of universities, meritocracy versus inclusiveness, and who should wield power over the curriculum, students, and the cultural agenda for society.

Patricia Marchak presents a remarkably fair and balanced account of the events. In a documentary-style narrative she reports the circumstances and gives a sympathetic reading to the very different perceptions of what happened. The focus is on the wider social and cultural context that gave rise to this painful episode.

Racism, Sexism, and the University is not simply about specific events at a particular institution. The issues addressed here are vital to universities everywhere; the political science affair at UBC brings them to the fore in a wide-ranging and hard-hitting debate.

M. PATRICIA MARCHAK is professor of sociology, University of British Columbia.

Racism, Sexism, and the University

The Political Science Affair at the University of British Columbia

M. PATRICIA MARCHAK

McGill-Queen's University Press
Montreal & Kingston • London • Buffalo

© McGill-Queen's University Press 1996
ISBN 0-7735-1514-3 (cloth)
ISBN 0-7735-1515-1 (paper)

Legal deposit fourth quarter 1996
Bibliothèque nationale du Québec

Printed in Canada on acid-free paper

McGill-Queen's University Press is grateful to
the Canada Council for support of its
publishing program.

Canadian Cataloguing in Publication Data

Marchak, M. Patricia, 1936–
Racism, sexism, and the university :
the political science affair at the University of
British Columbia
Includes bibliographical references.
ISBN 0-7735-1514-3 (bound). –
ISBN 0-7735-1515-1 (pbk.)
1. Discrimination in higher education – British
Columbia – Vancouver – Case studies. 2. Sex
discrimination in higher education – British
Columbia – Vancouver – Case studies.
3. University of British Columbia. Department
of Political Science. 1. Title.
LC212.3.C32B75 1996   370.19'342
C96-990008-2

Typeset in Sabon 10/12
by Caractéra inc., Quebec City

Contents

Tables and Figures

Acknowledgments

I want to thank a number of dear friends, though I shall not name them here, who helped me cope with the events, especially during a part of the summer when I reaped a whirlwind after sowing dissent. As well, I want to express my deep respect and gratitude to the faculty members in the Faculty of Arts who, in overwhelming numbers, understood that this was a serious matter that touched them at the core of their scholarly identities. My thanks also to Carlotta Lemieux, superb copyeditor, and to Joan McGilvray, managing editor at McGill-Queen's Press, for their care and understanding. To all those, whether they agreed with me or not, who engaged in a deep and civil debate over conflicting principles, I dedicate the book.

Racism, Sexism, and the University

CHAPTER ONE

Introduction

Five students presented a memorandum labelled "confidential" to the dean of the Faculty of Graduate Studies at the University of British Columbia in June 1992. It purported to represent the experiences of twelve graduate students in the Department of Political Science. It charged the department with "profound sexism and racism," discrimination, and violation of student rights. This was the first in a series of anonymous allegations against the department.

The data on grades and nominations for awards did not appear to substantiate claims of discrimination, but the students persisted. Eventually, the university commissioned an inquiry by Vancouver lawyer Joan McEwen to look into their allegations. Her *Report in Respect of the Political Science Department of the University of British Columbia* (1995), hereafter referred to as the Report, supported the students and was immediately adopted by the university president. Its recommendations were implemented, including the suspension of graduate admissions to the Department of Political Science.

These developments drew wide attention to both the Department of Political Science and the Faculty of Graduate Studies (FoGS). There ensued a prolonged and bitter nationwide debate about racism, sexism, and what some of the Report's critics called McCarthyism in Canadian universities. The furore was attributable in part to the Report itself; even its staunchest defenders agreed that it was seriously flawed. But while the Report was deplorable and was the cause of the immediate furore, the prolonged debate that followed publication outstripped the offending document. It signalled a sharp disagreement across campuses and in the public forum about the moral and intellectual issues implicit in the allegations and the university's response. The debates were superficially about the meaning of sexism and racism, but they were more centrally about the nature and purpose of universities, about meritocracy against inclusiveness, and about who should wield power over the curriculum, over persons, and over the cultural agenda for society.

None of the people involved in the affair declared that they were in favour of sexism or racism, and the debate was not about whether such repugnant behaviour was acceptable. No one wanted to be sexist or racist, no one wanted to defend sexist and racist behaviour, and no one wanted a neighbour or colleague to exhibit such behaviour. There were no charges of seduction or rape or promises of grades in return for sexual favours,[1] or anything more overtly sexual than a male professor hugging a female student instead of politely greeting her after a summer's absence. This is not a sordid story of physical abuse, and there are no scandalous sex scenes in it. However, buried in a mass of allegations, there were some about male professors making crude sexist remarks or attempting to "chat up" or arrange dates with female students. Other accusations were about "marginalizing" behaviour on the part of professors or male students, behaviour that sidelined women or put them in an inferior position. Accusations of harm, in the sense of causing differences in either the performance of students or the evaluations of professors, were included.

If these incidents occurred as reported, they constituted sexism as this is defined within current university policies and in human rights legislation applicable in British Columbia. Sexism may be defined as behaviour or institutional and cultural patterns that disadvantage and/ or discriminate against persons on the basis of sex without reasonable justification. As defined in the 1994 *Report on Human Rights in B.C.*, discrimination without reasonable justification may be intentional or unintentional, affects both individuals and groups, imposes burdens, obligations, or disadvantages based on prejudice or stereotypes, and can be caused by policies and activities that exclude persons on grounds other than performance or capability. Harassment is a type of discrimination involving hostile physical, visual, or verbal behaviour against an individual or group. As described by UBC's "Policy on Discrimination and Harassment," it causes physical, emotional, and economic injury to those it targets, poisons the study environment, demonstrates disrespect for individuals, and inhibits full participation in work and study opportunities.[2]

The graduate students who complained to the dean of FoGS claimed that they had been harassed and were victims of discrimination. In 1992, issues related to sexual harassment, employment equity, and multiculturalism were handled by separate university officers. Shortly before the inquiry was established, the university centralized these various functions under a new associate vice-president, Equity. Policies relevant to this case were being developed in the early 1990s, and they were more firmly embedded in university governance by 1994. However, by 1994 the publicity surrounding these complaints, combined with at least one student's rejection of university procedures in the Sexual Harassment Policy Office, led the administrators to appoint an external investigator rather than making full use of the existing channels for dealing with the charges.

On the allegations of sexism, the issue was not so much whether the alleged incidents constituted a crime, but whether, when all were put together, they constituted a crime worthy of all the noise and the penalty imposed. Sceptics asked, Were the unwanted flirtations so dreadful? And did the reported classroom incidents really marginalize female students, or were they misinterpreted and possibly overstated? On the other hand, supporters of the students affirmed that unwanted glances and suggestive invitations are serious offences and that forms of behaviour that marginalize women, although subtle, are nonetheless real and threatening. So this was a debate over process and interpretations rather than over facts or definitions.

The debate over racism was more difficult to decipher. A few complaints were about professors who made comments about other countries or peoples, or introduced metaphors or words to which someone in the class took offence on the grounds of racism. Whether these actually constituted racism was open to debate. Racism may be defined as behaviour that disadvantages and/or discriminates on the basis of attributes of race and/or ethnicity without reasonable cause. While there are two easily identified sexes and a limited number of gender orientations, there are no generally accepted criteria for identifying races. The physical attributes of the Canadian population are extremely diverse, and there are infinite variations in ethnic cultures. Racism is thus a more complex issue than sexism, though in both ordinary practice and human rights legislation Canadians recognize and prohibit harassment and discrimination against individuals and groups on the basis of physical or cultural characteristics. However, the B.C. Civil Liberties Association reviewed the Report and flatly stated that there was no evidence of racism.

But the graduate students and Ms McEwen insisted that racism was fundamental to the case. In one of the two opening memoranda, the students took this position:

The first symptom of racism is to deny that it exists. This is a feature of the way that racism is legitimated: by silence and a refusal to acknowledge that it is part and parcel of many ways of thinking and hierarchical assumptions about differences between people ... Nothing less than zero tolerance of racism will create an environment that is equally responsive, hospitable and intellectually engaging for *all* students and faculty. (8)*

Included in this argument was a denunciation of the term "ethnicity":

An informed and critical approach to raising questions of racism in which notions of "race" must be distinguished from covert or cosmetic terminology such as "ethnicity" is required. Students have been on the receiving end of avoidance tactics in which some faculty try to excuse their own or another's racism and/or sexism by calling it a "natural" problem of "cultural background." (8–9)

These comments were repeated in the McEwen Report, and the operational meaning of race was clarified: it referred to skin pigmentation. Two races were identified throughout the text: "white" and "persons of colour." Those labelled "white" were accused of racism. Skin colour became a euphemism for an implied history and culture attributed to all persons possessing the same skin pigmentation. The one exception to this was the frequent reference to persons who were Jewish.

The labelling by pigmentation became part of the heated debate. In defence of the students' point of view, three leading feminist scholars published an article which referred by skin colour to those whom they opposed. Although agreeing with critics who appealed to such core values of the university as knowledge, pluralism, tolerance, and mutual respect,[3] they argued that these values had been "historically employed to exclude and marginalize disadvantaged groups including women, people of color, native people and gays and lesbians." They continued:

On campuses across the country some professors are striving to protect their monopoly of power, the academic version of divine right. Again and again we hear the voices of white male professors claiming persecution by "intemperate" women and people of color. In these tirades, white males remain the universal unmarked standard of discourse and behavior. Every one else, it seems, is engaged in narrow, self-interest, "identity politics." These professors ignore their own history of privilege and the benefits they have received from exclusionary practices and, instead, expropriate the language of victimization.

Demands for more inclusive universities, which practise the pluralism they preach, threaten the faculty's right to unilaterally set curricula and research agendas without regard to consequences in the classroom or the perpetuation of partial understandings.[4]

---

* Page numbers in parentheses refer to the Report.

Towards the conclusion of the battle, the dean of FoGS, a champion of the graduate students who had lodged the allegations, argued in similar vein in a widely distributed public statement: "Until relatively recently, Universities have been dominated by senior white male faculty members. It is not surprising, but unacceptable, for this group to seek to perpetuate its domination of our University." He warned that removal of the suspension would inform students that faculty privilege was impeding their access to a hospitable learning environment; further, that one had only to consider the "demographics" of the contending groups to see the justice of his claim. The demographics referred to the skin colour and sex characteristics of those who had put forward a motion to lift the suspension (they were "white" and male).

These strongly worded inputs and warnings suggest that the persistent use of skin colour to mean race was intentional. The students specifically denounced ethnicity as an appropriate term, even though it, more than race, refers to culture and shared histories. The position appeared to be that all persons with "white" skins are one race and share a single dominating culture, while all others belong to a subjugated race that is fighting for its rights.

Because the skin-colour reference permeates this debate, we need to pause for a moment to consider who belongs in which group. If "whites" are categorized as all those who have immigrated from Europe or are descended from European immigrants, they include southern Europeans, who are often darker skinned than Asians, and people as diverse in cultural origins as the Portuguese and Norwegians. Although the complainants made it clear that they did not want culture included in the definition of race, McEwen, the feminist scholars, and the dean of FoGS clearly intended usage of the term to imply a history owned by all "whites" regardless of class, actual biographies, or nationalities. One could hardly doubt that the history was one of imperialism and colonialism, genocide, and class oppression. Yet this group included the losers as well as the winners in European history.

Those who were called "persons of colour" also came from many different sources: the entire continent of Africa (though where Europeans had maintained purity of skin colour, one supposes they would be excluded); Latin America (again, the precise boundary for colour and white became blurred); India and the rest of South Asia; China, Japan, and the whole of East Asia (but what does one do with the descendants of Dutch and Malay, or Chinese and Scots?); the non-European Mediterranean countries; and the continent of North America. Like the "white" label, the "persons of colour" label lumps together the winners and losers of history, the oppressors and the oppressed. Their only common link is that they are not "white."

Race and sex are the keys to reading the Report. The complaints recorded in it concern the behaviour of faculty members and "white" male students, and the curriculum and theories taught in the classroom, but in all cases they are viewed through the prism of race and sex. The students did not complain that the curriculum was outdated or irrelevant; they complained that "white" males taught an outdated and irrelevant curriculum. "White" males were accused of exercising privileges and rights that could no longer be tolerated by the "persons of colour" or those who chose to speak on their behalf. In particular, these critics questioned their right to establish the curriculum, evaluate performance, assess capacities; their right to engage in gate keeping for the profession, for the future; and their right to determine what constituted acceptable communication skills for graduate work. These were the sensitive issues at stake.

The challenge was mounted: Who should have the power to select readings, set assignments, and create academic standards? The complainants and their defenders argued that the curriculum and academic standards marginalized non-"white" persons and cultures. These marginalizing standards included requirements for communication or other intellectual skills which served as a handicap to those from certain cultures, and a bias towards certain kinds of approach to the subject matter, or styles of expression, which some women believed disadvantaged them; a bias towards American theoretical perspectives; interpretations of non-American cultures through a North American lens; and uncritical versions of the distribution of wealth and power among human societies or within Canada. All these matters were recognized as evidence of racism and sexism.

Professors have always assumed that the right to express their views in a classroom is subject not to current moral versions of the world but to canons of evidence and logical argument. This right is what tenure is supposed to protect, and it is the heart of academic freedom. It was thus inevitable that the arguments linking racism and sexism to classroom behaviour and the curriculum clashed with the tradition of academic freedom. There were accusations against the proponents of the suspension that they were "practising censorship and 're-education' reminiscent of the Chinese Cultural Revolution."[5] While such accusations were overheated, so were some of the defences. One student argued that professors whom the students found wanting should either be dismissed or be put into "re-education" classes.[6]

When one examines the allegations about what these particular professors said, one is frankly hard pressed to discover anything that seriously challenged the moral codes of contemporary society. What the students were challenging was not something the faculty said that was contrary to social norms but the uncritical adoption by faculty of society's opinions. Some complainants took the view that capitalist, patriarchal society was immoral to begin with and that professors did not offer critical views of it – did not, for example, teach feminist or neo-Marxist theory. At the same time, the criticisms seldom revealed to the earnest reader how, precisely, the offensive comments actually perpetuated racism, sexism, or homophobia, or otherwise marginalized students or enhanced the power of faculty members. This struggle over the meaning of pluralism, tolerance, and mutual respect was carried on at a level of abstraction that was often far above the realities of the department under scrutiny or the report on its activities.

The McEwen Report was itself a cause of much of the furore, because it treated the accused as guilty without a trial. It repeated all the allegations but investigated none; it said, essentially, that where there is smoke there is fire. All complaints were expressed in detail, and protracted complaints by a very few individuals were spread throughout the 178-page report as if they represented a cast of thousands. Contrary views from other graduate students, past and present, were omitted altogether or given short shrift. The context of events as seen by faculty or as factually ascertainable was omitted. Faculty responses – though faculty were interviewed at astonishing length and frequency – were relegated to a four-page appendix. The head of the department was gratuitously belittled and demeaned.

The investigator herself introduced sexism and racism into the Report by persistently categorizing individuals as "female," "white," or "Jewish" when these categories had no relevance to the statements in which they were embedded; for example, a "white male" faculty member would be accused of saying this and that to a "Jewish female student," even though the this and that had nothing to do with either gender or ethnic/religious positions. The implication was that the remark had some sexist or racist aspect, and thus the faculty member was damned by innuendo. Hence the Report became an issue unto itself, and it was the subject of much of the national debate.

However, the unfortunate McEwen Report was not the whole story. The students had other powerful supporters who, like McEwen, accepted all the accusations uncritically. One of these supporters was UBC's president, who said he believed that faculty and students must have equal rights to speak freely, otherwise academic freedom would be meaningless. He thought that the inequality of power disadvantaged students and was unjust, and he said he supported the complainants for that reason.

The inequality of power between faculty and students is indeed built into university organization. It could be removed only if faculty ceased to have the right to establish a curriculum and evaluate the performance of students. One supposes that the president did not intend to follow the argument to its logical conclusion, yet freedom to speak would not by itself be sufficient to meet the test of equality, no matter how tolerant and mutually respectful everyone was. The president did not suggest that faculty abandon their privileged control of classrooms or cease to select texts and give lectures. His comments apparently referred only to the freedom of speech aspect of equity. Since the complainants said they did not feel free to speak up, his protection may have been necessary. But faculty were not protesting against students' speaking rights. Nor was that concern central to the critique of the three leading feminist scholars quoted above or of Ms McEwen. Their concern had a much larger historical sweep to it and was about the power to act as well as speak.

A group calling itself the Coalition for an Inclusive University was successful in getting some three hundred signatories to its petitions. Inclusiveness became the shibboleth of the day. The petition invited all "who are committed to creating a healthy and open environment" to sign and support the president's "efforts to address issues of racism and sexism." This was sophisticated political action. One failed to sign at one's peril. Who could oppose a healthy environment? Equally sophisticated political action produced several letters from external groups in support of the president or the graduate students. Those who mounted this campaign were politically smart even though, like their opponents, they were a coalition of groups that might otherwise have been uncomfortable in one another's company.

The opposition to the penalties imposed (though not necessarily to inclusiveness, whatever its definition) was not united. Its component groups would not likely have been compatible political allies. Some characterized the whole affair as political correctness and used such terms as "McCarthyism" and "Salem witch trials." Some were opposed on the grounds that academic freedom was being violated: faculty members should not be subjected to moral censure for what they said in class or for the academic standards they established. Others were opposed on the grounds that the compendium of complaints as stated in the Report was a mountain of trivia, that nothing there constituted grounds for suspension of graduate admissions. Some thought that although the complaints may have been serious, they had little to do with sexism and racism. Many more were opposed on the grounds of process: they held that the inquiry and the resulting report were in violation of natural justice, or due process. I include myself among the last of these groups (and not among its erstwhile allies), and at this point I must interrupt the narrative to inform the readers about the person writing this chronicle.

I was the dean of arts at the University of British Columbia in the period that encompassed the political science affair. I was one of two deans who commissioned the inquiry, and I was one of the half-dozen or so administrators who drew up the "terms of reference" and appointed Ms McEwen to the investigation. I accept my full share of responsibility for "being there," though (as is always the case) hindsight is a much better guide to what we ought to have done than any guide we had available at the time.

I will not accept responsibility for the direction the investigation took, for the investigator's failure to consult with the professors emeriti who had agreed to act as consultants, her failure to complete the investigation in a reasonable time, the extraordinary cost of the undertaking, the report that was finally produced, the UBC president's adoption of the report, or the enormous harm that was done by it. I had no control over these matters.

But I do not write by way of accepting or absolving myself from blame. There were enough axes ground at the time, and this is not another contribution to the collection. I believe that the issues raised in the political science affair are of concern to universities everywhere; the particulars become one case study in a proliferation of such events. The events should be recorded and analysed while they remain fresh in our minds; but, more than this, the underlying issues, the more philosophical concerns about the nature of a university, the meaning of equity, and the nature of a multicultural society deserve continuing discussion.

This book is both a narrative about the political science affair at UBC and an exploration of the moral and intellectual issues it raised. It is not, repeat, not an exposé. It is not an axe grinder. It most certainly is not a character assassination or a taking of sides, except in defence of due process and with respect to rational intellectual discourse. It defends neither the complainants nor the accused, and may well make both of them unhappy. Although it is written by an insider who had access to private conversations and files, the documentary information contained here has already been published or been widely disseminated, except with respect to a couple of items that I myself authored, and an occasional reference to the contributions of others, who have given their permission to be quoted. I have not taken advantage of privileged sources – a mild irony, because under the British Columbia

Freedom of Information and Protection of Privacy Act, complete strangers have access to confidential information.

I believe that the issues debated in this affair are absolutely central to universities in the closing years of this century. They include the pitting of feminism and multiculturalism against tolerance and academic freedom; the meaning of due process, or natural justice, in the face of allegations about a "chilly climate" for women; and – if it does not sound too grandiose – the value of the Western rationalist tradition versus popular postmodernism. None of the positions is clearly a winner; there is something to be said on both or all sides. My objective is to explore these issues and to examine the "case" – the political science affair – in the light of them.

I realize that some eyebrows will lift and noses twitch at the notion of a former dean, moreover one who accepts some responsibility for the turn of events, telling the tale. My response is that I am first of all a scholar, a sociologist by training, and I take the scholarly role seriously. Universities have become impossible bureaucracies where deans have ceased to be academic leaders. I am choosing to write this tale because I think it has more to do with what is happening at universities today than all the fundraising boosterism that deans are now obliged to undertake. The issues here matter, and how universities deal with them over the next decade may well determine the fate of the institutions themselves.

I also write as a feminist who is deeply concerned about the claims being made in the name of feminism. Equity requires some levelling of the ground and legal protections for women, but its achievement will not be enhanced by treating allegations against men as proof of guilt. Those who want to champion women's right to equal opportunity and treatment are ill advised when they treat claims against men as being true by fiat. The advancement of women – and also the maintenance of universities – rests on a system of well-considered ground rules that are fully respected and observed during both peaceful and troubled times. I write, then, because in my view this inquiry employed unjust procedures. I cannot go along with those who, in the name of feminism or through sympathy with those who claimed victimhood, supported the judgment because the accused fitted the stereotype of "white men."

Finally, I write because, as one who cherishes the multicultural texture of my society and whose personal life and biography reflect my joy that I live at this confluence of many cultural streams, I am profoundly disturbed by those who would divide the human species into "white" and "of colour" (or any other simple-minded and, from my perspective, racist categories). That Europeans in the age of imperialism committed sins against humanity does not confer on those who live in postcolonial times the right to discriminate against persons with blond skins any more than against persons with black, brown, or buff skins. I cannot admire the descendants of those Europeans who, perhaps believing that they can undo history by taking on the guilt of their ancestors, divide humankind by skin colour.

A fair amount of grandstanding punctuated the debate on the political science affair. There were eloquent speeches by the proponents of academic freedom, intellectual pluralism, and ideological tolerance; there were impassioned speeches by the defenders of women and minority groups against bigotry and discrimination. There were also administrators who wanted to appear to be leaders in the transformation of universities and who used such words as "inclusiveness" without apparently being aware that these terms either had no meaning or were inconsistent with other messages on behalf of meritocracy which these same individuals were pronouncing. There was no intellectual leadership from the central administration, though there was plenty of political posturing. And as is always the case in such politically charged events, there were many who straddled the fence, either in the hope that they could remain on good terms with all the protagonists or simply because they were too bewildered to sort out the issues.

I spoke strongly against the way the inquiry was progressing when it became clear to me that the investigator we had appointed was intolerant of views that were divergent to her prejudices, but I was unable to interrupt a process that should have taken a month and instead took ten months. On receipt of the Report, I offered my resignation as dean on two grounds: that I was named in it as a negligent administrator and that I found it a disgraceful document which, as an administrator and as a female member of the faculty, I could not support. My resignation was turned down, but I informed the president immediately that much as I respected his motives and person, I could not be a team player on this one; that if he insisted on imposing punishment on the basis of the Report, I could not remain a silent witness.

It is in line with this declaration that I acted throughout the affair and in the writing of this book. I have written it in an academic mode; in other words, I have done my best to narrate the events and quote the actors fairly. Since any document must involve selection of facts and personal interpretations, I cannot claim some miraculous objectivity, but I can say that I have made every attempt to provide a fair and balanced version of the events. The reader, now forewarned of my administrative role and my philosophical stance, is free to judge the success of my offering.

The book is organized as follows. Chapter 2 is about the intellectual and ideological debates at universities in the 1990s, and also about the changing sex ratios and other demographic conditions that provide the context for such affairs as the one at UBC. The issues in the intellectual debate are germane to the political science affair because what some reformers demand is a reformulation of the mission of universities. This demand is based on the argument that there is no truth to be pursued by intellectual exercise – that all histories and arguments are rooted in the gender, ethnic, class, and other identities of their proponents.

The next five chapters address the specific allegations, the quantitative data referring to them, the investigation procedures, the McEwen Report, and the reactions to the Report. Chapter 3 provides details of the allegations made by graduate students before the investigation, including those that were general and those that named errant faculty members. Chapter 4 looks at a range of quantitative data on admissions, withdrawals, grades, and nominations for awards, and at student surveys conducted in the period under review. It concludes with lengthy excerpts from external (academic) reviews of the department. Chapter 5 examines the terms of reference, the process envisioned by the administration, the number of students interviewed, and the public comments of students and faculty who were interviewed but not represented in the Report; it also comments on the interviewing techniques, on external critics of the process, and on Ms McEwen's defence of her method.

Chapter 6 presents the key allegations as reported by Ms McEwen; much of this is given in her own words and in the format she chose. The chapter concludes with the recommendations and their immediate acceptance by the president. Chapter 7 provides a wide-ranging review of the public commentary following the president's decision, and gives a chronological account of the battle during the next several months. I have not included every single incident or public comment, of course, but I have tried to represent a range of opinions in the original words of the speakers or writers.

Chapter 8 provides my own critical assessment of the report. Here I take it literally, without considering its underlying messages or total context. There is no deconstruction. I consider each group of allegations and the context and evidence, where possible. Since all that we have are allegations and since these have rarely been matched against the evidence or examined in context, we can only read the text and eventually make decisions about specific allegations on the basis of a preponderence of probabilities.

Finally, chapter 9 stands back from the Report and the particulars of this affair to consider once again the social and intellectual issues that it raised. Where the Victorian author Matthew Arnold could advocate sweetness and light as if the two were inseparable components of wisdom, we are confronted with conflicting claims on behalf of moral purity and intellectual rigour. Does it make sense to see the role of the university as the pursuit of truth or as the advocacy of good causes? Are meritocracy and inclusiveness mutually incompatible? I suggest that if universities are no longer able to defend the tradition of disengaged inquiry in the pursuit of objective truth, if they no longer believe in that tradition, then their identity is at stake. That tradition is what defines them; without it, they are indistinguishable from any other institution or any other way of learning and disseminating information. We are certainly at a juncture at the end of this century, and the strongest forces separating universities from that tradition emanate from within.

CHAPTER TWO

Ideas of a University

Racism and sexism are big words in this tale of alleged wrongdoing in the Political Science Department at UBC. But are they the whole tale? I think not. Many of the accusations against faculty were about control of the curriculum and the evaluation process. People wanted to be included in the intellectual establishment and they believed they were excluded. According to the McEwen Report, they believed that their exclusion was because of their sex or race, or both. But while focusing on these personal attributes they were also arguing that the curriculum, the intellectual approach, the kind of training their teachers had undergone – and sometimes the entire university structure – obstructed their opportunities. For their part, faculty members argued that they were objective in their evaluations, that personal attributes were irrelevant, and that in many cases the complaints were contrary to the spirit of a liberal education.

Here lay the problem. The defenders and detractors of the McEwen Report had totally different notions of what intellectual life was about, and the differences were not trivial. This chapter is concerned with the differences. Readers who want to get to the facts of the case can skip to the next chapter, but I warn them, they won't make good sense of the story if they ignore its intellectual and ideological context.

IS OBJECTIVITY POSSIBLE?

Universities are founded on two central ideas. One is that truth exists independent of human perceptions of it. The second is that in seeking truth, the personal characteristics of the seeker are irrelevant. These two ideas have motivated scholars for some eight hundred years, and long before the first universities were established in Europe the same ideas were formulated by Greek philosophers. It is still these two ideas that make the university a unique institution throughout the world. These ideas may be labelled realism or the Western rationalist tradition.

The popular campus challenge to this traditional version of the enterprise argues that all knowledge is political, gendered, and ethnocentric, and that all pursuits reflect the social values and status of the seekers. There is no external objective reality. These views have been expressed in various ways throughout modern history but in contemporary form are often labelled postmodernism, or deconstructionism. Popular versions of postmodernism, as of most other isms, are not necessarily consistent with the arguments of the philosophers who generated the ideas.

If one takes the rationalist position, it is perfectly reasonable to evaluate the efforts of students and colleagues on a set of criteria deemed to be objective. If they master the experiment or comprehend the poem, it matters not a whit whether their skin is one colour or another. And if they make an argument that displays ignorance of the accumulated knowledge, it may be a silly argument irrespective of their sex or orientation. Note that the word here was "ignorance": one is permitted, encouraged, and applauded for offering an argument with explanatory power that is superior to those in the bin of accumulated knowedge so long as the novel approach is based on evidence and logic.

If one takes the postmodernist position, however, the situation is not so easily resolved. Who chooses the criteria? Who determines whether the experiment has been conducted or the poem comprehended? It matters a good deal whether the skin is one colour or another, because those with one colour might think differently from the others about the experiments or poems. As to accumulated knowledge, or what scholars these days call the canon, well, who did the accumulating? Who selected what was to be included or excluded? Who decided that history happened this way or that, that this philosophy is worth knowing but that one is worthless? Everything becomes very personal, because subjective criteria are the only criteria available if one takes this approach.

The Western rationalist tradition is the philosophical framework for modern science. It posits an independent reality or truth, and the objective is to find what scientists call a correspondence to that reality. They do this by undertaking repetitive and rule-bound experiments to test various hypotheses. The hypotheses are rooted in rigorous, logical argument, not in intuition, revelation, or faith. Researchers test hypotheses that contradict their theories as well as those they think are true, to ensure that they do not simply confirm their personal beliefs. If these null hypotheses (as contrary ones are called) turn out to explain the data better than the favoured theories, the researcher is obliged to make that information public and revise her theories. The mind-set for scientists is scepticism, and their objective is knowledge rather than confirmation of faith.

The rationalist position has had a long run. Even the major critical theories over the past couple of centuries were rooted in the rationalist position. Marx's critique of capitalism, for the prime example, raised no objections to the scientific method or to science itself; on the contrary, it utilized and praised both. For generations of scholars, the notion of truth was genuinely held, and truth was sharply distinguished from belief, just as the scientific method was distinguished from advocacy. The cultivated mind might want both to seek truth and to advocate goodness, but it knew the difference.

As a defender of the rationalist tradition, John R. Searle is currently at the front of a contemporary battle line in universities. He has emphasized that in seeking objective knowledge, scientists do not engage in *ad hominem* or what philosophers call "genetic" arguments. He has observed that science cannot and does not offer conclusions or tell us what to believe. It simply tells us what one might conclude if a set of assumptions were true and if the supporting evidence were sufficient. In one of his articles, Searle argued against turning intellectual inquiry into a political ploy. Such a ploy was evident, he suggested, in a statement by a group called the American Council of Learned Societies, which claimed that "as the most powerful modern philosophies and theories have been demonstrating, claims of disinterest, objectivity and universality are not to be trusted, and themselves tend to reflect local historical conditions."[1] In Searle's terms, "intellectual standards are not up for grabs." While we might not arrive at the conclusion of a debate, neither would we accept just any argument, *ad hominem* arguments, or miscellaneous ideas in place of logical argument: the rules are explicit and firm for the disinterested scholar to develop a universally valid representation of objective truth.

Postmodernism is less easily stated in brief terms, both because different proponents have diverse interpretations of its central tenets and because its popular version (much in evidence at UBC during this time) and its intellectual formulations are not coincidental.[2] Contemporary philosophers of science in this mode include Thomas Kuhn and Richard Rorty, who have argued that science does not create more probable or better approximations to the truth, but rather that human minds and their capacity for communication penetrate all reality. The correspondence we seek is not to external but to internal and communicatively shared realities. Kuhn's interpretation of the history of science indicates that scientific revolutions occur at the stage where an accumulation of evidence refutes existing explanations and finally pushes sceptical minds to reformulate the entire theoretical approach. His understanding of this is that it is not an external truth that is involved in the revolution so much as a change in the way that engaged scientists collectively agree to formulate the problem.[3]

In lectures delivered at UBC in March 1994, Richard Rorty disputed Searle's arguments on knowledge as objective representations of reality.[4] He noted that philosophers interested in democratic politics said that the search for truth would lead to a more equitable and inclusive community because it generated tolerance and rationality. He suggested that truth was an unnecessary postulate for purposes of generating tolerance and rationality; a search for social agreement or justification would be equally appropriate. Science, in his view, as in Kuhn's, actually seeks a social consensus on what exists or on what to believe. This line of argument includes the recommendation that intellectual ambitions should be restated in terms of human relations rather than being stated in terms of human relations to non-human reality (as in the notion of truth embodied in the natural sciences or in theology).

Rorty disagreed with Searle on whether the normal practices of universities were seriously threatened by such philosophers as himself, but he did not condone and was not a supporter of those who would convert academic departments into political power bases. He suggested that those who use his work, or that of Jacques Derrida and Kuhn, to legitimate the abandonment of all rationalist methodology are confused about the argument.

Subtle distinctions, however, are not the stuff of the debate raging on the campuses where deconstructionism and postmodernism are taken to mean the jettisoning of all notions of objectivity and disinterested pursuit of knowledge. In the popular version, the goal of the academy is not the gathering of knowledge so much as the use of it for political purposes: the university becomes a centre of advocacy research and of the dissemination of (politically interested) ideas. Instead of remaining a centre for managing the status quo, it can be transformed into a centre for revolution, working towards the transformation of the Western tradition and patriarchy.

In this approach, there can be no disinterested scholarship – no objectivity, no universality, no truth beyond human versions of it. At the popular level, some who call themselves postmodernists accept no standards of scholarship. If all scholarly work is political, gendered, and ethnocentric, then no objective standards can be established. To paraphrase Nietzsche (who has re-emerged as an intellectually defensible figure, having been buried since his adoption by nazism in the 1930s), there are no facts, just interpretations. For some, any interpretation is as good as any other.

But if intellectual life is nothing more than interpretation, why should a society maintain expensive universities? Those who wish to use the university as the base for transforming society may have a ready answer. Transformation has a certain consistency with the moral purposes to which universities have been harnessed throughout modern history. But society at large may want to consider whether the vast research capacities of universities are best employed in a revolutionary campaign. In any event, citizens would want to ask what transformations are envisioned. The overthrow of patriarchy is a major one according to some advocates of change; the overthrow of "white" culture likewise. Searle takes a dim view of the enterprise:

Tradition is an obstacle in their path. In spite of their variety, most of the challengers to the traditional conception of education correctly perceive that if they are forced to conduct academic life according to a set of rules determined by constraints of truth, objectivity, clarity, rationality, logic, and the brute existence of the real world, their task is made more difficult, perhaps impossible. For example, if you think that the purpose of teaching the history of the past is to achieve social and political transformation of the present, then the traditional canons of historical scholarship – the canons of objectivity, evidence, close attention to the facts, and above all, truth – can sometimes seem an unnecessary and oppressive regime that stands in the way of achieving more important social objectives.[5]

I have outlined these two approaches in minimum detail and offered them in contrast to one another so that their differences can be recognized. Naturally, there is more to their respective positions, and there is a history of development for these ideas. Some of the faculty members and students who engaged in the debates on the political science affair at UBC were well acquainted with the philosophical literature and chose their words carefully. Others were less familiar with the intellectual arguments and spoke from their hearts. What came into the debate was not reference to the philosophers of science but assumptions about the world – that objectivity was or was not possible, and that intellectual activity had nothing or everything to do with the genetic composition of the speaker.

FEMINISM, CIVIL RIGHTS, AND OTHER LIBERATION MOVEMENTS

Liberation movements emerged throughout the world in the postwar era. Colonialism, the subjugation of minorities and women, and prejudice against gay and lesbian people all came under attack. The civil rights movement in the United States became a major process of transformation for Afro-Americans. The feminist movement re-emerged stronger than than ever before. These were all part of the context for what was happening at universities in the 1990s, by which time postmodernism, or popular versions of it, were also providing some of the intellectual and ideological justification for the direction these movements were taking.

The feminist movement underwent considerable change as it gathered momentum in the postwar period. Equity was what feminism was all about in the century between 1870 and 1970. In the immediate postwar years, as increasing numbers of women moved into paid work and institutions of higher learning, equity meant equal opportunities for grades, employment, wages, and promotion; it was straightforward. But as time passed, it became evident that equity was not enough if the rules of the game were stacked against women. The only way they could enter a field dominated by men was to have the recruitment criteria changed, and the only way they could advance was to have positive promotion policies in place. More than that, they needed some clear prohibitions and penalties placed on any man who either discriminated against them or treated them as playthings, and they needed equity in the kitchen and in child rearing. To prove discrimination or crude behaviour was no easy task, but many women – who were now in sufficient numbers in offices and factories to make their voices heard – began to document the hurdles that interrupted their progress. They demanded what is now called inclusiveness – systemic conditions that remove obstacles (intended or otherwise) that discriminate against women. The objective of most women in the 1990s was still equity, but the understanding of equity had evolved from its simple beginnings, and at the same time some feminists were reaching the conclusion that equity in any form was not enough.

Simple equity was not the message of some leading feminists from the 1960s onwards. Kate Millet's *Sexual Politics*[6] opened the contemporary debate with the argument that male hegemony and sexual domination permeated all the institutions of Western industrial society. Gloria Steinem, Carolyn Heilbrun, Catharine MacKinnon, and many "new" or "gender" feminist theorists who followed their lead have concentrated on the history and contemporary expressions of patriarchy and gender exploitation. They hold that mere equity is inadequate because the institutions are permeated with patriarchal versions of the world and with practices that destroy women; indeed, destroy humanity and the earth. The goal for those who share this view is the elimination of patriarchy, that is, the transformation of society.

Arguments in this vein tend to concentrate on Western society, which is regarded by some feminists as especially patriarchal. Patriarchal understandings of the world permeate much of liberal secular society – for example, legal systems and processes designed by men; science that has devoted itself to the exploitation of the earth; and linear, logical thought processes that lend themselves to science and legal systems. Transformation, then, may require that science, legal systems, secular society, and all that is part of the Western *Weltanschauung* be swept away.

Transformation is envisioned in these formulations as a cultural rather than economic process. Rarely does anyone invoke Marx or neo-Marxist theories of transformation. The objections to capitalism are phrased not in terms of class or class struggle but in terms of the struggles for recognition and equality for racial minorities, women, gay and lesbian people, and other persons who are victims and oppressed members of society. The new feminism links up with other angry movements in contemporary North American society. Indeed, the same writers are central to social movements in all the English-speaking countries, and to lesser degree elsewhere. American gender feminists may be part of the intellectual baggage for any woman of the 1990s, empowering her to feel angry with justification; the bloody-minded world is given a villain in the form not only of living men but, even more, in the form of enduring and oppressive patriarchy. In a patriarchy, women are always victims; men, always oppressors.

In the universities, feminism became popular and entrenched in women's studies and other programs from about the 1970s onward. Leading academics condemned the institutions that now employed them for having failed for so long to include women and minorities. During a debate on the UBC political science affair, historian Veronica Strong-Boag provided just such a condemnation. First, she described the monastic traditions of Christian patriarchy and the development of sectarian universities that failed to support the interests of women and the poor, and she then turned to contemporary academic institutions, which have

helped to rationalize imperialism, capitalism, racism, and sexism in the service of Europe's and North America's expansionary states. As in the earlier universities, there have been dissenters from conventional wisdom. Internal critics have challenged white, male, and middle-class privilege in and outside of the academy. Their observations have rarely been welcome. Right from its 19th century beginnings, academic freedom has not been for every professor or student. Persecution of those who championed the equality of the sexes, the classes, and the races has been commonplace.[7]

"New" or "gender" feminists were important academic leaders in the evolution of women's studies during the 1980s and 1990s. But contrary arguments are now emerging, as in a recent publication by Christina Hoff Sommers. Her argument is that gender feminists have exaggerated the evil of men, inflated statistics on such matters as rape and wife battering, and harmed women by treating them as inevitable victims. As a feminist, she objects. She characterizes tenured professors at prestigious universities who become "engaged and enraged" new feminists as "articulate, prone to self-dramatization, and chronically offended."[8] The gender feminists might well point out, in rebuttal, that most tenured professors at prestigious universities are still men, many of whom are also articulate, prone to self-dramatization, and chronically offended. Be that as it may, gender feminism and equity feminism have become divisions within the feminist movement, and these differences are part of the culture of universities.

In addition to differences of opinion on patriarchy and revolution, feminism is a less cohesive movement today than in the 1970s because differences in perceptions and definitions of self-interest are becoming evident on several fronts: between lesbian and heterosexual women, by generation, and along ethnic lines. The radical feminists of a generation past are regarded as "new Victorians," according to one young writer.[9] She holds that they have marginalized feminism and turned it into a sexually repressive instrument that encourages women to be victims. The ethnic issue is largely one of salience. The question might be: Is gender the most important division in society, or is race more important? This is not an academic question. It is one that affects the fundamental concerns of women whose ethnic characteristics differ. It is probably the central division of the feminist movement and the one most capable of destroying unity among women.

Whatever intellectual position women may choose, they are likely to have certain experiences in common. These might include coping with unwanted and even violent sexual advances by men, dealing with teachers or others who pay more attention to male students, and responding to men who treat them as sex objects. Some have been denied jobs or other opportunities because of their sex. Experiences such as these predispose a woman to believe other women's allegations of sexual improprieties or discrimination. In a university setting, where faculty members are still predominantly male but more than half and up to two-thirds of the students are women, women are more likely than in the past to express their anger and frustration when encountering sexism. Thus, feminism and also other liberation movements, especially in combination with postmodernism and deconstructionism, are powerful instruments for social change in universities.

SWEETNESS AND LIGHT

Universities are unique because of the rationalist tradition. But throughout their history, another tradition has also infused their culture. It is a voice urging teachers and students alike to seek not merely truth but wisdom; and not merely scientific knowledge but moral goodness. Cardinal Newman's mid-nineteenth-century essay on the university[10] has been read by generations of students, whether to inform them of the meaning of a liberal education or to whet their appetite for graceful prose. Newman argued that the university brought together "an assemblage of learned men," each knowledgeable in a branch of science, who through their obligatory interactions came to respect one another's subjects. They created an intellectual climate characterized by tolerance for ideas and a thirst for knowledge. His learned men are now learned women and men. With that needed corrective, his message is still relevant:

[A student] apprehends the great outlines of knowledge, the principles on which it rests, the scale of its parts, its lights and its shades, its great points and its little, as he otherwise cannot apprehend them. Hence it is that his education is called "Liberal." A habit of mind is formed which lasts through life, of which the attributes are, freedom, equitableness, calmness, moderation, and wisdom; or what I ... call a philosophical habit. This I would assign as the special fruit of the education furnished at a University, as contrasted with other places of teaching or modes of teaching. This is the main purpose of University in its treatment of its students.

Newman argued that knowledge was capable of being its own end, its own reward; that the meaning of the word "liberal" was that it was not servile, which he understood to mean "bodily labour, mechanical employment, and the like, in which the mind has little or no part." Thus, "liberal education and liberal pursuits are exercises of mind, of reason, of reflection."

Another Victorian, Matthew Arnold, provided the most frequently cited words on culture, "not as having its origin in curiosity, but as having its origin in the love of perfection; it is a study of perfection." By extension, universities, which were then becoming important to the development and sustenance of the culture of industrial societies, were encouraged to add the study of perfection to the search for truth. Culture, said Arnold, "moves by the force, not merely or primarily of the scientific passion for pure knowledge, but also of the moral and social passion for doing good. The pursuit of perfection, then, is the pursuit of sweetness and light. He who works for sweetness and light, works to make reason and the will of God prevail." Arnold warned that sometimes the "passion for doing good" could be "overhasty" because its motive force was action rather than thought, and reason had to intervene to effect a proper balance: "What distinguishes culture is, that it is possessed by the scientific passion as well as by the passion of doing good."[11]

Arnold's vision has been shared by many humanists during the century since he so eloquently expressed it, but in the late twentieth century his critics have dismissed him as an upper-middle-class male whose identity and interests advanced the imperialist spirit of his age. Even so, his notion of a liberal education has managed to survive. It joined the objective pursuit of truth with conscientious devotion to doing good, and the ancient Greek notion of wisdom which combined truth and virtue was thus reintroduced to modern society. Methodist and Presbyterian ministers supplied later generations (some of whose members still teach and preach in such places as the University of British Columbia) with plentiful notions of goodness to supplement scientific rigour. The notion of doing good has often been translated in the modern university as the creation of good citizens. Creating citizens became a central purpose of a liberal education during the democratic twentieth century; and creating equity for all citizens became a major additional purpose towards the end of the century. This was all very well, but what happens when science and a particular version of moral goodness clash? What happens when good people equally devoted to moral highroads are travelling down different roads? In the 1990s there have been many such clashes, and the political science affair at UBC was one of them.

ACADEMIC FREEDOM

The traditional values of a university – following on the rationalist tradition, the early religious influences, and Victorian concerns about wisdom and goodness – are tolerance for diverse opinion, pluralism, and freedom of intellectual inquiry. The general rationale for nurturing these values is that we do not know the truth; we merely seek to know it. Thus, we must allow all voices to speak. There cannot be a single orthodoxy in an intellectual environment.

These values, however, all rest on the assumption that everyone already understands that ideas must be tested by some standard and that if they fail the test they will be discarded; and on other assumptions, such as that ideas are independent of their bearers. This approach is not consistent with contemporary postmodernism or feminism, or with various other isms that are current on university campuses. Identity politics, as some of the isms are now called by opponents, promote the interests of their members rather than standards devised by others (particularly others who are unlike the members in identity). Having given an audience to Dr Strong-Boag's view of the university, let us also listen to one of her strongest opponents during the political science affair, Philip Resnick:

There is a real danger that the adherents of various forms of identity politics may seek to elevate their particular approach to the status of an orthodoxy and to impose it as the underlying principle that must govern all university activities, all forms of research and teaching. The so-called inclusive university that certain of these groups claim to pursue may turn out to be anything but inclusive. For it threatens to exclude any and all who might challenge or question its adherents' beliefs. In short, it threatens to turn the university into an illiberal institution.

A liberal university must allow free expression to a broad range of opinions. Its members, while free to differ with one another in their points of view, need to share allegiance to the same rules of openness, pluralism and fair play. And no group must be allowed to claim some monopoly position on what is virtuous or true.[12]

THE UNIVERSITY AS MERITOCRACY

Universities are not egalitarian communities. Scholars who have passed certain tests rank above those who have not done so or who have not yet gained the requisite credentials. There are senior and junior scholars, teachers and students, and even the students are divided by the degree of immersion. There are tests to gain entry and tests to gain honourable exits. Although individuals are not equals, defenders of the organization would argue that there is equity built into the standards for entry and exit in the form of identical tests irrespective of personal attributes. This defence begs two questions asked by critics: whether equitable standards mean equality of access when there are diverse pre-entry situations; and whether equity is achieved when the competing populations differ in cultural understandings and values.

The tests themselves may pose a separate problem. They must be objective so that the personal characteristics of competitors are self-evidently irrelevant. The natural sciences might claim that a test of mastery is objective and that both the student and the judge would know whether an experiment or body of information had been mastered at the end of the day. The test in the liberal arts is more ambiguous. Does one really understand a poem? Has one fully comprehended a text? Has one communicated one's understanding with sufficient eloquence? Determining that a student has achieved mastery of a field in the humanities or social sciences inevitably involves social consensus rather than obvious and entirely objective truth; the student has mastered the field if a committee of teachers or a department of colleagues agrees this is so. And what if the candidate, the writer, and the committee differ in gender, class, ethnicity? Would they then share interpretations, and what would constitute a disinterested or objective test?

We would be closing our eyes to history were we to believe that women, working-class people, and members of minority groups had equal access and promotion opportunities in practice. Still, enough people of nonprivileged origins did gain entry and move up the university ladders to justify the meritocratic ideology. Universities became the avenues for the advancement of people from nonprivileged origins. Other employers came to depend on universities to do the sifting and sorting; they reaped the benefits of graduates guaranteed to have passed certain standard requirements. Those who failed at university, as a consequence, lost other opportunities as well. Meritocracy, then, became a means of excluding as well as including aspiring participants in the wider society, inevitably generating hostility in the process.

TWO UNIVERSITY CULTURES

The science establishment tends to go about its business in laboratories and classrooms without much discussion of wisdom and goodness, but the humanities and social sciences are unable to avoid such big issues.[13] Social scientists can rarely engage in controlled experiments, and they are obliged to confront insoluble puzzles about the nature of humanity and human societies with little more than crude methods and imagination. It is true that there are insoluble problems in science too and that many problems are beyond current methods of study. But the condition that is endemic in the social sciences and humanities is less pervasive in the physical sciences. In consequence, the science establishment at universities is generally comfortable with the Western rationalist tradition. Although some physical scientists occasionally speculate about theories of chaos and uncertainty, neither postmodernism nor other counter arguments have had much effect on the everyday conduct of science.

Although the social sciences are at a disadvantage, they have been established on the same objective basis as the sciences. Practitioners are expected to respect data and to seek out disconfirming as well as confirming evidence for their ideas. They are obliged to become familiar with accumulated work in their area and to respect the contributions of others. There are conventions, methodologies, classical literatures, and rules for the conduct of research. All of this, of course, is contrary to the spirit of popular postmodernism, and while the sciences slumber on unaware that they are contravening postmodernist understandings, the social sciences and humanities are unable to provide equivalent proof that their rationalist traditions result in incontrovertible knowledge.

In addition, the social sciences and humanities are concerned with the condition of human beings and societies. While some practitioners may be able to keep the subject matter at a distance – treating voting patterns, revolutions, state terrorism, political leadership, and social movements such as feminism or the anti-apartheid movement as the counterparts to chemicals, genes, or amoeba – many find it impossible to maintain a distance between themselves and their subject matter. If they are studying a particular society or organization, they cannot avoid becoming familiar with the actors (even when the actors are historical figures). If they study economic development, ideologies, social movements, or oppression, it is extremely difficult to treat evidence impartially and without regard to the social implications. Some subjects are so dicey that social scientists refrain from publishing their findings because publication could harm innocent or vulnerable people. Obviously, these subjects are unlike the physical sciences.

Further, it is obvious – and one needs no lessons in postmodernism to observe it – that national and local conditions affect the development of intellectual inquiry. The discipline of political science is an outstanding example. It is a quintessentially American product imported to Canadian universities where it displaced departments of political economy or became one of the new departments that descended from combined social science organizations. These changes occurred when both faculty and student populations expanded during the postwar boom. Because Canadian universities had not yet established graduate programs, the teachers had degrees from British and American universities and there were more of the latter than the former. Those with American degrees taught a curriculum similar to that of the major American universities. This included a theoretical approach known as pluralism, which treated power as a negotiated outcome of the competing interest groups and institutional sectors in society. American approaches tended to ignore or downplay the relationship between economy and polity, did not pay much attention to the study of class structure or class dynamics, and focused on contemporary works more than on the classical literature in political philosophy. In these respects the American approaches to the study of politics differed from those of continental Europe and Britain.

During the postwar boom, when most political science departments were being established or were experiencing rapid growth, the university was undergoing a major transformation. Where it had earlier provided a liberal education and professional training for the sons and a few daughters of the well-to-do, it was now expected to educate the progeny of a rapidly expanding middle class. Small departments that had revelled in the mystique of their calling were transformed into large organizations teaching hundreds of undergraduates. Mystiques and callings quickly gave way to mass-produced survey texts and ordinary jobs. Education and job training ceased to be distinguishable, and those fusty scholars who still thought in terms of the scholarly community and such high-minded (and elitist) concepts as the cultivation of the intellect and the pursuit of perfection were persistently shocked by the (democratic) factory in which they actually worked.

By the late 1960s, Canadian universities were beginning to establish their own graduate programs. In these, as in American universities, hundreds of students prolonged their immersion in higher education in the hope of obtaining the credentials that would turn them into permanent academics. This democratization of universities spread the wealth of education but simultaneously diluted its market value. It provided the mobility route for children of the less well-to-do, and in many cases it was they who eventually staffed the universities, because they became devoted to the institution that had given them these opportunities. It provided the equalization route for women as well. In a country that was now absorbing more immigrants from non-European sources and in a city that was en route to being predominantly Asian, the University of British Columbia was an exciting multicultural experience during this growth period. All of these undoubted benefits came with the downside. Where a BA or BSc degree had been the gateway to heaven for graduates of the 1950s, by the 1970s one needed at least an MA to pass Go and collect $200. By the 1980s, employers in the most diverse markets deemed a PhD to be a reasonable entry-level demand. The credentials mill ground out the graduates, and the meaning of the whole activity became blurred.

Graduate student numbers increased rapidly at UBC after the mid-1980s, when the president issued a mission statement directing the university to become a research-oriented and graduate educational institution. In the sciences faculty members could subsidize tuition fees for their graduate students from research grants, but funding for research in the humanities or social sciences was scarce and students had little access to money. The number of students soon exceeded the available funding, and even with additional funds for teaching assistantships and scholarships, many students were not provided with enough money to see them through a year of studies. Nor was there adequate office and lab space, or any other provisions for the expanded intake.

In addition to the immediate shortfalls in funding, graduate students faced an uncertain future. Universities were now contracting, not expanding. Although UBC's Department of Political Science had a good record of placing its graduates, as their numbers increased both at UBC and across the country, their chances of obtaining a tenure-stream academic post diminished. Other employers were not plentiful either. The civil service jobs that had once absorbed any excess of graduates (indeed, of students with BA degrees) were also declining as one government after another faced debt crises and outraged taxpayers. Nor was the private sector demanding advanced degrees in political science. Thus, many of the students who entered graduate programs in political science (and most other humanities and social sciences) knew that they had no guarantee of subsequent employment or security.

One of the demographic changes in universities over the postwar period has been a dramatic reversal in the sex ratio. By the 1990s, about two-thirds of UBC arts undergraduate students, just over one-half of MA students, and one-third of PhD students were female. The proportions for political science were almost identical to those for the faculty as a whole. Male students are still more numerous in the sciences and in most applied sciences, but even there the proportion of women has steadily increased.

Equality of opportunity for women had been achieved, even exceeded, in the universities. But by the 1990s not only were academic and other employment opportunities diminishing (for both sexes), but so was funding for universities. One is reminded of an unpleasant fact of history: whenever women have attained a numerical majority in a field, the overall status and income of the field has declined. Two obvious examples are the clerical and teaching occupations. Attacks on the contemporary university and the erosion of public funding for it might also be read as a loss of interest by taxpayers and governments in an institution that now educates more women than men.

While women may read the declining fortunes of universities in the light of their own experience, there is in fact more to it than that. From the early 1980s to the mid-1990s, with the baby boom past and a shrinking economy, universities across North America have experienced budget cuts and shrinkage, as have all social services and institutions. Where universities once had a monopoly on higher education, on the training of scientists, and on scientific research, there are now alternatives: other institutions and technologies for delivering education, other institutions for undertaking research, and a proliferation of credentials that compete with and are already reducing the value of university degrees. Governments and taxpayers are losing interest in paying for mass education in these expensive institutions, and the games academics play have ceased to amuse the population at large. In this context, the popular press and even the tony magazines have taken turns in finding fault with universities, and especially with that part of them that has remained devoted to liberal education. In 1995 the B.C. Labour Force Development Board, representing business and unions, presented a major policy paper to the B.C. government advocating the redirection of funds from universities to vocational training schools.[14] Defences of liberal education fell on deaf ears: the board had a willing audience.

THE MARKET VERSION OF A UNIVERSITY

Between the great philosophical stances and beyond the social movements, there is a student-centred market conception of the university. It concerns how the university is viewed by the students who pass through it, by the taxpayers who support it, and by the economic interest groups – businesses, unions, governments – who define it in utilitarian terms. For a very long time, perhaps since universities began to be public institutions connected in some way to the marketplace, students have viewed these institutions as a source of credentials that gave them a leg up in life. Thus, the meritocratic principle was essential. But as fees increased and as universities and colleges became more competitive for student dollars, the language of the marketplace became more common on the campus.

Initially, students became clients. The client model encourages them to be active participants in their own education, and it sits comfortably with prevailing academic standards. The customer model, which soon became more prevalent, is another matter. Customers are not evaluated. The point is to sell them something and make them want it and like it so that they or their sisters will return for more. Customers are always right, and they cannot be failed. The argument currently made for this approach has no philosophical foundations. It simply assumes that universities have to satisfy their customers, without really considering whether satisfaction has any relationship to truth, objectivity, canons of argument, and all the other criteria by which faculty have traditionally evaluated students. The customer view of the university fits in with popular postmodernism, less because of a philosophical agreement than because universities have, almost without noticing it, shifted away from the Western tradition of rationalism and the meritocracy embedded in it. Many of their administrators (now often professional managers rather than academics) have no idea what it is they are throwing out. Other administrators have ceased to believe in objective academic standards; they agree with those students who say that the standards make sense only for an already privileged group.

The student-as-customer and credentialism-as-education views of university functions blend nicely into demands for more work-related

skills training and less liberal arts. When the B.C. Labour Force
Development Board suggested redirecting funds from universities to
vocational schools, one of its arguments was that this would benefit
the multicultural clientele. Decoded (to use an "in" word), this meant
that students whose first language was not English would be better off
learning a trade. It was also a recognition that universities – especially
that part of them devoted to transmitting the Western literary tradition
in the liberal arts – were limited in their capacity to teach an increasingly multilingual population.

TRADITION AND SOCIAL CHANGE

Those who share the belief that universities have historically defended
privilege, class oppression, exclusiveness, and gender inequity may
prefer to have universities closed. If universities have, as they claim,
sustained patriarchy, imperialism, and anti-human sciences, the institutions may have blocked progressive social change. Such views are
expressed by those who divide the population of the university, as well
as the Western world, into "white" and "of colour," men and women,
others and ourselves. Yet these voices have privileged access to university classrooms and are respectfully heard. Their owners have followers
and they are free to argue their case in public forums.

They coexist with scientists who are blissfully unaware that a debate
over their activities is taking place, and with opposing voices who
argue that history has many more features to it, that bifurcation of
humanity diminishes the rich complexity of the species, and that it is
possible to engage in a disinterested search for truth and knowledge.

The defenders of the university, of whom I am one, argue that these
unique institutions are capable of accommodating such sharply divergent perspectives because they long ago established tolerance and
mutual respect as their cultural values. Those who attack the university
argue that the institutions merely absorb and deflect criticism and thus
actually thwart essential social change. As well, they argue that those
who defend the institution are holders of power and thus are merely
defending their own interests. Most holders of power are male and
"white," so when one of them, such as myself, turns up in other guise,
the explanation is that we are colonized; we have internalized our own
victimization; we have, as it were, joined the enemy. Power corrupts,
yet the critics of the contemporary university most earnestly seek their
share of it. Social change for them necessarily reverses the current
order: they, instead of "white" males, would organize the curriculum,
select the readings (or abandon readings in favour of oral traditions,

perhaps), and teach a new generation of students very different versions of history, philosophy, and science.

I understand the political science affair as part of a social and intellectual movement to change the direction of the university fundamentally and radically. If this understanding is correct, the university community needs to engage fully in the discussion about conflicting objectives and their relative merits. To engage only when an eruption occurs, as when a department is under seige, is naive: the moral high ground in such a battle is already captured by those who claim they have been ill-treated, and the debate does not occur in an open and tolerant arena. Both sides become heated, and truth (at least for those who believe in it) is the inevitable casualty. The time to engage in the debate and to insist that all the interests and objectives be explicit is during the quiet period.

The central issues are clear enough. Should we sustain universities as truth-seeking organizations? Should they continue to operate on traditional meritocratic principles for entry and advancement? Can equity and meritocracy coexist? And can we continue to be tolerant of both the traditional disciplines (which might be male-voiced and Eurocentric) and the critical alternatives (which might be female-voiced and otherwise biased)?

CHAPTER THREE

Anonymous Allegations

Philosophical arguments about the meaning of the university may seem removed from the allegations mounted in the political science affair, but they, and the general economic and social context of the university, were always part of the story. This chapter begins the narrative about the events themselves. For the moment, I shall keep the other concerns as a backdrop. (Note: All page numbers shown in parentheses refer to the McEwen Report.)

INITIAL ALLEGATIONS, JUNE 1992

According to the allegations initially presented to the dean of the Faculty of Graduate Studies (FOGS) in June 1992,[1] male faculty in the Department of Political Science were biased and unfair in their treatment of women students (2–4, 34–5, and much of chap. 4). They were unsupportive, obstructionist, and unprofessional in their dealings with female students. The students said that they were treated with hostility when they tried to address these issues within the department, and they expressed the belief that they would be harmed if they were identified. They said that there was "a profound problem with" sexism and racism. Their allegations included the following:

- that there was a dramatic (relative) decline in the number of female PhD students;
- that faculty expressed intolerance of ideological pluralism;
- that faculty had a "parochial attitude toward women, visible minorities, and international students";
- that women students were given an unequal burden of teaching assistantship work;
- that faculty showed favouritism towards some students;

- that rules and guidelines were not clearly articulated;
- that the department was misrepresented in its recruitment materials; and
- that students had no formal input into hiring practices.

Response of the Department Head to the June 1992 Allegations
(4–5, 35–6)

The initial memorandum was labelled "confidential," and when the dean sent it to the head of the department, he counselled extreme confidentiality in dealing with it. The department head's response to this letter expressed surprise at the allegations. He regarded the language as "inflammatory, if not slanderous," and he found some charges to be "exaggerated, misleading, or simply untrue." He said that, to his knowledge, no previous complaints about sexism and racism had been made and that none of the concerns had been expressed in departmental meetings or other forums. He acknowledged that "this department, as is true of many if not most political science departments in Canada is overwhelmingly male and white. Given limited hiring opportunities it has been difficult for us to alter this balance. It is probably true that some of us are not as sensitive as we should be to issues of gender and race. However, the record will simply not sustain charges such as 'sexual terrorism' or 'systemic racism.'"

The department head also denied the allegations of discrimination. He noted that in thirteen graduate seminars in the year identified in one of the complaints, women students had finished at the top or tied for first place in eight. He pointed out that half of all PhD students at that time were non-Canadian, and one-third of new entrants in that year were women, and he thought that, proportionately, women held more fellowships than men. He specifically and strongly rejected some claims, such as the statement that "graduate students have no formal input in the hiring practices, politics or decisions of the department." Students, he said, had been put on hiring committees following a resolution of the university senate in 1991 (the resolution was brought to senate by a faculty member in political science); they were also represented on other committees of the department. He also rejected the claim of misrepresentation in recruitment advertising.

Nevertheless, the department head agreed to bring the problems to the attention of his faculty. He acknowledged a "problem of graduate student perception and morale which must be addressed," and he promised to do so "to the best of my ability." However, he observed: "That job is not made any easier by the circulation of complaints which may be legitimate together with slanders, baseless accusations and half-truths. Racism and sexism are serious issues. This University has established procedures to deal with them which are designed not only to protect the victim but also to safeguard the rights of those who are falsely accused. I do not understand why, to my knowlege, those procedures were not utilized" (4). The McEwen Report is highly selective in its summary of the department head's rebuttal of the charges of racism. However, because I will not quote correspondence which although official is private, I can only indicate that he had much more to say by way of refuting the charges.

After an exchange of letters, the dean of FoGS met with the head of the department and the graduate adviser in October 1992. The dean was given copies of departmental brochures that had been sent to graduate students describing programs, procedures, and policies; as well, he was given a list of activities the department was undertaking to deal with the perceptions of the critical students. The department undertook a number of internal changes during the year following the complaints. These included the establishment of committees to review and make recommendations for change in the PhD program, in the undergraduate curriculum, and in the organization of the department more generally.

These responses did not satisfy some of the complainants or the dean of FoGS. According to the McEwen Report, two female students sought to withdraw (one permanently, the other temporarily) in October 1993, and their complaints led the FoGS dean to contact one of the complainants of the previous year, a student who had transferred to another department after failing her comprehensive examinations in political science. The dean informed her that there were "continuing problems in the Department of Political Science leading to the withdrawal of several women graduate students," and he invited her and other students to meet with him and prepare a memorandum about their "perceptions and continuing problems" (43). This they agreed to do.

In addition, a spokesperson for the students drafted a memorandum of understanding, which contained four conditions the students required:

- an acknowledgment of discriminatory bias and/or inappropriate behaviour with respect to the department's handling of its graduate students and/or the administration of the graduate program;
- an acknowledgment that options existed for handling/resolving some of the student concerns in cooperation with the Faculty of Graduate Studies;
- a statement that further contributions from the students would be required, including a detailed account of their concerns and their

suggestions towards setting an agenda, as well as an indication regarding further student involvement; and

- an acknowledgment that FoGS would continue to assist students, on an individual basis, in resolving outstanding obstacles to the completion of their degrees (44).

The dean agreed to the last three items but pointed out that there would have to be an investigation before agreement could be given for the first. On this basis the students wrote a second memorandum to the department.

THE SECOND MEMORANDUM, 15 NOVEMBER 1993 (5–10, 44–6)

The students' second memorandum, coming out of this collaboration with the dean of FoGS, claimed to speak not only for the original twelve students but for another six as well. It said that not all faculty were equally guilty and that the concerns were caused by "only fourteen faculty members in the Department." At the same time, it rejected or discounted the measures the head of the department had taken the previous year, as well as the department's efforts to deal with earlier criticism. It stated:

- The head's letter had mentioned a decision taken at a departmental retreat to "more aggressively mentor" new students; the term "aggressive" was "inappropriate."[2]
- The department had not made explicit and public the fact that students had complained of faculty members' behaviour, and any actions that faculty had taken were not explicitly in response to the complaints. Faculty had failed to respond to student concerns that had been raised in the department through all available channels, and they had persistently denied that there were problems. They treated complaints as "perceptions" or "imagining things."
- Nothing the department had done dealt with the issue of racism or gender bias.
- There had been no response to or investigation of resignations of female students from the program.
- There were negative attitudes towards the academic work of students "whose first language may not be a European language."

As with the first letter, much of the anger was about the program and aspects of the departmental organization of graduate studies, but perceived inadequacies in this respect were said to be particularly burdensome for students who did not fit the mainstream and needed more mentoring or information than other students. The overlap between criticism of academic programs and charges of sexism and racism was contained in comments about the hostility expressed by some faculty members towards non-Western perspectives, including the work of social and political theorists outside the Western tradition. As well, the students expressed some disdain for professors who claimed to teach feminist theory or gender studies in their courses but were not doing it well.

The strongest criticism was of exclusionary or marginalizing behaviour, as in such incidents as faculty giving less consulting time to women or expending less effort in intellectual discussion with them. As well, the students complained of racist comments in seminars, either by faculty (examples given: "Gentlemen prefer blondes" and "[East] Indians are chauvinists") or by fellow students. They argued that faculty should have stopped students who made such comments. There was specific criticism of an alleged departmental practice of requesting photographs on admission, indicating that physical attributes constitute part of the criteria for admission. On the delicate issue of racism, the students criticized the department for a lack of graduate courses on the subject. In a lengthy discourse on this issue, they put forward an argument that was later repeated, apparently with approval, by McEwen. This was the statement beginning "The first symptom of racism is to deny that it exists," which I quoted in chapter 1.

The students said that they had been asked by the dean of FoGS to "contribute to a course of action to address the concerns," but they felt that they had done everything in their power to encourage reforms and nothing had happened. Thus, they thought it pointless to engage in further faculty-student discussions. They claimed that some undergraduate students shared their concerns, and they asked the dean of FoGS to meet with faculty and ensure that all faculty members were aware of the events and issues (45).

Departmental Responses, November 1993 and April 1994

On receipt of these new allegations, the head of the department responded to the dean of FoGS on 19 November 1993, as follows (46–9):

- A female appointee to faculty had not been prohibited from teaching graduate students, as claimed; she had started her job too late to be assigned a graduate seminar or new students.
- Students were not asked to supply photographs prior to admission. The request for photographs and for responses to a questionnaire had been mailed in May 1993 (whereas admissions are undertaken between October and February); the material was in fact required

for a "Who's Who" in the department. (The head enclosed a copy of the request.)

- The students' memo had included extracts from students' letters about grading practices in three separate appendices. The head stated that these all came from one single letter which, together with the supervisor's response, was on file in the department.
- Changes had been made in departmental policies in response to the concerns raised by students, and the head outlined these changes.
- There had been no appreciable change in the rate of resignations from the program; the statistics remained better than the average for the Faculty of Arts. Detailed data on admissions, withdrawals, grades, and awards were provided to the dean and later to Ms McEwen. (These details are shown in the next chapter.)

At the same time, the department head indicated that he and the department were prepared to undertake discussions, alter procedures and policies, and make whatever changes in the graduate program would be conducive to an improved learning environment. He communicated the concerns of the students in a memo and department meeting of 23 November, and he outlined interim measures to improve the relations between students and faculty in a memo addressed to both dated 15 December 1993.

A few months later, on 5 April 1994, the department head reported to the dean of FoGS that the Department of Political Science had undertaken a survey of faculty and graduate student opinion on issues related to the graduate curriculum and the social climate; that students and faculty were in the process of developing a grievance procedure; and that a committee to review administrative procedures in the graduate program had been established. He noted that the intention to invite a specialist on race relations to meet with the department had been put on hold because a visit might be construed as a violation of due process with respect to a case then resting with the UBC Sexual Harassment Policy Office. This case is described below. He also observed:

There is a down side to all this which I should have anticipated earlier. By informing all graduate students and faculty about the concerns of a minority of students, albeit an intense minority, without revealing the details of the student memo which I was directed to treat as confidential, I had hoped to clear the air and assure students of the good intentions of the faculty. This probably helped to some extent. On the other hand, it has left us wide open to accusations that any decisions with negative consequences for women or minorities must be racially motivated or the product of sexism. (63–4 and the original document, quoted with permission)

The head expressed his frustration at being required to respond to anonymous accusations and complaints and said it was his belief that one or more of the complainants might have "deliberately included false or misleading information" (64). He added: "Insofar as the accusation rests on the two specific cases mentioned in the last graduate student memo, there is no basis for them, and neither student has ever proceeded to use the appeal procedure which was specifically offered to them" (63).

On 6 April 1994 the department adopted a formal "student grievance procedure," which was described in its preamble as "an attempt to resolve disputes as close to the source as possible" rather than as a replacement for any existing university documents.

NAMING OF ACCUSED

The dean of FoGS had urged the students to put their complaints in writing, and they had done so, but the substance continued to be treated as confidential. Indeed, the directives to the head of the department required confidentiality and discretion in order to protect the students, yet simultaneously it demanded action and responses from the accused. Faculty were not named in the two memoranda, and although some could easily be identified, others could not, even by their colleagues.

In the spring of 1994, some students decided to move into another phase: to name individuals and make formal accusations against them to the Sexual Harassment Policy Office on campus and to the teaching assistants' union, one of the staff unions, the B.C. Council of Human Rights, the mass media, and a few other organizations and individuals. Although the accused were named, the students naming them remained anonymous except where they chose to make themselves known. Much of the information on these charges came from the Sexual Harassment Policy Office or from the dean of FoGS, and both enjoined faculty members to treat it as confidential even when the complainants were acting very publicly. The first public case, which was reported by McEwen and repeated in the mass media, concerns a complaint against a faculty member who called one graduate student "a big bad black bitch."

The "Big Bad Black Bitch" Case (50–6)

This case, which will be referred to as the Jones case, has been widely reported in the media. Both the complainant and the professor have been identified by name in press reports, and the complainant has circulated her complaints both on and off campus, so there is no legal reason to give her an alias. However, since my objective is to explore the nature of events rather than to identify individuals, she will be Jones and the professor, Bonet. No symbolic meaning is attached to either name: I chose them simply as neutral tags, no more.

The apparently noncontroversial "facts" are as follows. A non-Caucasian female student, Ms Jones, hired as a teaching assistant by the department and working under the supervision of a male Caucasian sessional lecturer,[3] Dr Bonet, filed a complaint with the Sexual Harassment Policy Office on campus charging her supervisor with racism for calling her a "big bad black bitch." Bonet, on receiving notification of the complaint, apologized in writing "sincerely and without reservation." He offered an alternative interpretation of the event, but asked her forgiveness for "my insensitivity."

According to Jones in her letter of 21 March 1994 to the Sexual Harassment Policy Office, she and Bonet had been walking towards his office, and she had been telling him how her assignment of low grades to a few undergraduate males in her course section had gained her some respect from them. Professor Bonet had replied, "Now they know you are a big bad black bitch." Jones's letter described other incidents which she felt were also cause for complaint. In his apology, Dr Bonet said that the offensive words had been part of a jocular exchange, which had followed Jones's expression of concern over whether she had been too tough on the students. He disputed making the comment as she phrased it, but he conceded that the comment he had made "was clearly in poor taste," and he offered his apologies.

The head of the department also offered "sincere regret" to Ms Jones, in writing, and assured her that the faculty member had been formally reprimanded. He made arrangements for her to submit her essay to another teacher, to submit grades for her students to himself directly, and in other respects to avoid all contact with Bonet. Ms Jones wanted further assurances, however, and complained that his first letter had been too concerned with her distress rather than with the offender's behaviour. So the head wrote a second letter of apology a month later. In it, he informed Ms Jones that he had distributed copies of a research report entitled "The Classroom Climate: A Chilly One for Women" to all faculty members and graduate students, and that he was inviting specialists on equity issues to work with the department. Acknowledging that Bonet's behaviour was wrong, he said, "We failed to provide you with a work and study environment free from harassment and must strive harder to remedy the situation" (51).

These letters were believed by faculty to have been distributed to some other students by Ms Jones. Several faculty members and students were aware of a rumour that they were to be used as evidence of a "confession," with the purpose of destroying the department. The head expressed concern about his legal position and that of the university. He also expressed concern for Dr Bonet, about whom rumours had been so widely circulated that the head of the Department of Political Science at the University of Toronto had phoned to make inquiries. It subsequently transpired that Ms Jones had sent copies of her ultimatum letter (discussed below) to the dean at Toronto as well as to many others. Bonet's wife was a PhD student in the Department of Political Science at Toronto.

It was coincidental that this was Bonet's final year of teaching in a sessional capacity at UBC. He had been given advance warning the previous summer; the reason was budgetary and had nothing to do with the case. On 28 March 1994 a delegation of undergraduate students who had no connection with the case visited me, as the dean of arts, to ask the university for an extension of Bonet's employment because they found him a very good teacher. According to a letter of 5 April 1994, which the head of the department wrote to me (and which largely dealt with the positive steps the department was taking to deal with the problems), most members of this delegation were women, many were members of visible minorities, and one was "in the forefront of activity to combat racism on campus and in the wider community." These students were not at the time aware (and neither was I) of the Jones case in the Sexual Harassment Policy Office. Bonet's teaching assessments were entirely favourable. There was nothing on his record at any time prior to this event to suggest other than that he was a conscientious and capable teacher. This information was available to McEwen, but she did not include it in the Report.

Ms Jones claimed that two months after the fracas with Bonet, he and another political science professor harassed an undergraduate friend of hers "because he was seen with me." She said, "This incident caused a relapse in my recovery from the entire episode and has left me even angrier than I was previously." This encounter was the subject of further correspondence, with allegations on the one side and denials on the other, but since it is not germane to the allegations of sexism and racism, I shall not describe it further.

Fourteen Non-negotiable Requests, 23 June 1994 (52–3)

Ms Jones wanted more than an apology from the department. On 23 June 1994 she submitted a complaint against the entire faculty of the department to the Sexual Harassment Policy Office, with copies to a lawyer, the ombudsman's office, the teaching assistants' union, and several others. She concluded her letter with fourteen "non-negotiable" requests, including payment of $40,000 and threats to contact the media and many individuals and organizations external to UBC. A revised letter two weeks later repeated the conditions. Although many people have copies of these letters, I feel constrained to follow McEwen's very brief account. Thus, I shall omit the lengthy list of specific complaints against other members of the department besides Bonet. The non-negotiable requests included:

- guaranteed completion of the MA and unconditional acceptance into any political science department of comparable standing;
- $40,000 for refunded and continued tuition and expenses;
- the constitution of an unorthodox MA thesis committee that would include a geography professor and a PhD student in political science (Ms Keate, whose case is described farther on);
- on graduation, six letters of recommendation acceptable to her; and
- reassignment of grades for courses not passed.

As well as making these demands, Ms Jones offered an ultimatum. If she did not receive a letter of apology from Bonet (in addition to the one he had already given), she would contact the president of the University of Toronto to request that he ask Bonet's wife to obtain the promised apology; alternatively, she would contact the professor's wife herself. She further demanded that five professors (including one woman) be disciplined and that she receive copies of the reprimands; that any prospective employers of Bonet be warned of his problematic behaviour; and that various other disciplinary actions be taken. In addition, she said she must have time to recover from the trauma she had experienced, and she wanted the Sexual Harassment Policy Office to monitor all activities concerning herself and the department until she graduated. Finally, she wanted to ensure that the undergraduate student who she said had suffered recriminations as a result of being her friend would be protected. She concluded her letter by warning that if she received no response within eight working days, "legal action will ensue," and she would contact various media and other offices.

Responses from the Department Head and the Named Professors (54–6)

The department head responded to the dean of FoGS on 27 June 1994, providing a chronology of the events and rejecting the many charges in Jones's letter. The head pointed out that the original Bonet apology had been delivered to Jones within hours of receipt of her complaint and that she had given absolutely no indication of problems with other faculty prior to submitting the "expanded" complaint to the Sexual Harassment Policy Office. Referring to another issue she had raised in her lengthy letter, he noted that her application for graduate study had made no direct or indirect reference to a desire to pursue the political economy of China as a research focus (as she claimed in the letter). He said that all the documents she had submitted had referred to international relations as her field of interest.

The specific complaints against professors other than Bonet were examined with some difficulty, since the department head was initially obliged to maintain the anonymity of the complainant, while the complainant remained free to criticize faculty publicly. The named professors were not given voice in the McEwen text, though reference to their rebuttals and the head's acceptance of them is noted. This is one of the rare places in this book where I shall go beyond the McEwen text to cite their written responses.

The head talked with the professor (whom I shall call Professor A) who was alleged to have made the comments "Gentlemen prefer blondes" and "A pretty girl is like a melody." He reported that this individual agreed that he had used these and a couple of similar expressions. But he had done so as pedagogical devices to show how metaphor and hypothesis testing were employed in the development of comparative political theory. Professor A explained that he had moved on from comical to more sophisticated empirical examples, such as "Working-class people vote for left-wing parties." Having used this format in earlier classes, he was surprised that anyone should take offence, but he said he would refrain from using the phrases again.

Professor A was also accused of stating, "Blacks are at the bottom of the racial hierarchy." At first, he could not recognize this as his own statement, but it later occurred to him that he might have made some such remark during a seminar on South African apartheid – but as a description of the apartheid system, not as a normative statement. Professor A had taught the same graduate course for nearly ten years and had never previously been accused of sexism or racism. In the 1993 class, the national backgrounds of the students had included India, Pakistan, Japan, Israel, Britain, the United States, Hungary, and Canada. There were ten women and seven men enrolled. The professor said that Ms Jones had not at the time expressed any complaint to him and that in the intervening seven months before submitting her complaint, she had greeted and conversed with him whenever they met.

Similar responses were given by the other named professors. Their interpretations of the events were clearly at variance with those of the student. Some faculty members, including Professor A and at least one other named professor (Professor B), had at some earlier stage criticized Jones's written presentations. A further complaint came up on more than one occasion – that Jones had been told to take a specialized area-study undergraduate course before undertaking to write a thesis about China. One faculty member involved, Professor C, stated that he had advised her, just as he would others, to take advantage of this means of learning the basics before embarking on advanced work. His advice had certainly not been the put-down that she had interpreted it to be.

At the request of the department head, Jones met with him on 17 July 1994, but no resolution was achieved, and in a letter dated 18 July she informed him that she had sent everything to the head of the Department of Political Science at the University of Toronto, advising that it be forwarded to Bonet's wife. She then imposed a new deadline for dealing with her case – 25 July 1994 – which, if not met, would cause her to contact "other faculties on and off campus." Copies of this letter were sent in many directions.

The department head, having conferred with the deans and the vice-president, informed Ms Jones in writing on 29 July that the university would not provide financial compensation or meet the various other non-negotiable demands. He noted, "In order to deal with your concerns, this department has requested that the Dean of Arts and the Dean of Graduate Studies arrange for an independent inquiry into the department's treatment of women and minority students." This letter apparently crossed in the internal mail with one from Ms Jones to the head in which she rejected a decision by the Sexual Harassment Policy Office to refuse to take on the widened case against the whole department; in her view, the decision was an "act of corruption" (55). The letter continued for several pages and was copied to various university officers and also to persons outside the university.

Complaints against the Sexual Harassment Policy Office

According to McEwen's account, when Ms Jones widened her complaints by charging the whole department with sexism and racism, the adviser in the Sexual Harassment Policy Office informed her that she was confusing discrimination and academic concerns and that her complaint was more in the nature of a series of "personal" grievances than a systemic complaint against the whole department. The adviser said, "If you only want to criticize or present ultimatums to the department and the University, neither I nor the Sexual Harassment Policy Office are able to be much help. If you want to push the system to create a better situation for graduate students, including yourself, you can count on our support and assistance in creating and following an effective procedure to this end" (54).

This letter elicited the reaction cited above – Ms Jones's letter to the head, dated 28 July, in which she said that the adviser was engaging in "further victimization and an act of corruption." She also upped her demand for compensation. She said that unless she received a satisfactory response by 3 August, she would want $50,000 "for the additional stress and trauma" (55).

An Ex-Student's Input (56–60)

One of the authors of the 1992 memorandum, Ms Lane (an alias), who had since enrolled in a PhD program in the United States, wrote a confidential letter, dated 9 May 1994, to the dean of FoGS about her perception of sexism and racism in the department. She subsequently allowed the letter to be published by McEwen, so it has become part of the public record. Faculty members are named in this document, though the names were expunged in McEwen's published extracts. It is a lengthy discussion of Ms Lane's experiences and includes the following allegations:

- There was a significant disparity between the number of male and female students in the graduate program.
- The general attitude was that women were inferior.
- Male students had more access to faculty and interacted with them.
- Male students received favourable treatment, as reflected in the grades (considerable detail provided, with names in the original letter) and in the granting of extensions to deadlines.
- There was overt racial bias; "non-white people were often treated like second-class people."
- A named professor (whom I shall call Professor D) "clearly valued the comments made by male students more than those of female students," even though (in Ms Lane's recollection) there may have been more women than men in the class and there were at least four people who were members of minority groups. Professor D gave lower grades to women, and lower grades were given to women for the "participation" component of the grade, though women regularly attended classes and some men did not. "The minority students received as low or lower grades overall than the female students," though Ms Lane also mentioned that she alone, a female and a member of a minority group, had received a first-class grade. The

professor allowed extensions for paper submissions to men but not to women and "non-white" students.

- A named professor (Professor E) "continuously ignored or discounted" the opinions of "non-white students." As well, he made "personal comments about some students to other fellow students." He told some students that a certain "black" female student should not have been enrolled in graduate school because her work was of poor quality, and he was rude to the student herself.
- A named professor (Professor F) "had a well-known reputation among students for treating non-white students in a discriminatory manner," and consequently Ms Lane did not take courses from him "which would have benefited my work."
- A named professor (Professor G) accorded preferential treatment to attractive women. He "would often touch female students by putting his arm around them, patting their behind and, in at least one instance, he pulled a female student onto his lap!" (58).

Department Head's Responses, July 1994

The department head sent excerpts of the memorandum to the four named faculty members, and he sent his response to the dean of FOGS on 26 July 1994. "The statement about gender imbalance in the graduate program is incorrect," he told the dean. "The M.A. cohort has been at least 40% female since 1988. The figure for this academic year is 56.3%" (59–60). Regarding Professor D, he said he could not locate any class fitting the description given by Ms Lane (i.e., with more women, at least four minority students, and in which a female minority student had received the only first-class grade), and he provided the dean with the grade distribution for the years 1989–93 for the graduate class taught by Professor D. Since it it easier to read in tabular form, I reproduce it as table 1. The head said he saw no evidence of systemic discrimination against females or minority students in this distribution; he noted that in 1993 all three female students had earned A grades, one of them tying for the top grade in the seminar, and that in 1991 a minority female had received the second highest grade.

Ms Lane had also accused Professor E of discrimination. The years in which Ms Lane took courses from him were blocked out by the dean of FOGS in order to protect her identity, but the head deduced that 1992 must have been one of the years she was referring to. Yet Professor E was on release time (no teaching duties) that year and was on sabbatical leave the following year. His graduate seminar in 1991

Table 1
Grade distribution for one graduate class, by gender, 1989–1993

	Number of students				Graded A	
Year	Total	Minority	Female	Minority and female	Female	Minority
1993	8	2	3	0	3	0
1992	10	1	2	1	0	0
1991	13	3	4	2	2	1
1990	13	5	6	3	2	2
1989	8	1	2	1	0	0

Source: Professor's response to the department head's request for information, following complaint

had contained only one minority student, a female who had earned the top grade in the class. Ms Lane subsequently retracted her comments about Professor E, saying that she had had no firsthand dealings with him. Nonetheless, the complaint was printed by McEwen with the retraction in brackets (58). The information that the professor was not teaching at that time and that the previous year he had given the top grade to a minority female student was not reported.

The "Mature White" PhD Candidate (the Keate Case) (60–3)

Ms Keate (an alias) complained in January 1994 about a grade she had received in the fall 1993 term, and in March 1994 she expressed further dissatisfaction with the teacher as well as with the response of the head of the Department of Political Science. In April she raised various concerns about the department, about several of the professors, and about her fear that she was being "stereotyped" and "marginalized." She concluded: "I urge you, therefore, not to ignore or suppress my complaints that I am being isolated and marginalized intellectually. If the department (and Graduate Studies) cannot guarantee protection from these individuals, then it should shut down the Political Science graduate program until it has a new generation of faculty who understand that the days of hierarchy, competition and capricious wielding of tenure and grading power are over" (62).

Following this announcement, Ms Keate (who had negotiated a postponement of her comprehensive examinations until October 1995) castigated several faculty members by name. Since this lengthy letter was sent to the *Vancouver Sun* and the *Globe and Mail*, it may be in the public realm, but I will nonetheless cite only those portions of it repeated by McEwen.

Much of Ms Keate's anger was about a grade which she felt was unfair and which she attributed to "a major difference in political preferences" between herself and Professor H. She claimed that the professor's written comments were (I will use the moderate phrase in the Report) "unduly harsh." On receiving her complaint, the department head had informed her that she was entitled to seek an independent appraisal of the paper by a second member of faculty, one either inside or outside the department; and that if the grade assigned by this independent assessor proved to be significantly different, he would recommend a grade change. This procedure was then undertaken, and on the basis of the independent assessment the head advised Ms Keate that he would raise her grade. He informed the dean of FoGS that in his view "there was a genuine difference of opinion about the quality of the paper" and that the grade distribution for the seminar did not support the student's allegation of age and gender discrimination (60–1).

In her letter to the newspapers, Ms Keate said that the head had informed her that her specific grievances had been dealt with in accordance with established department and university procedures, but she said that these procedures did not impress her. She berated the head for regarding grievances as unfounded accusations; in her view, he had persistently treated faculty members as blameless. Further, she rebuked the UBC Sexual Harassment Policy Office, as well as the department and the Faculty of Graduate Studies, for failing to deal with "chilly climate" issues. According to Ms Keate, "No office exists which addresses the process by which a student's newly formed professional identity is deformed and destroyed ... What the male faculty absolutely refuse to share is their intellectual power and prestige" (67). She argued that the Sexual Harassment Policy Office was a component in "the diffusion process which stifles students who complain of this larger picture." Students, she said, try to describe the step-by-step creation of an intellectually hostile environment, but UBC policy forces them to "dismantle this holistic account into watertight situations examined as completely unconnected incidents. Unless an incident is then proven to contain direct sexual or racial assault in some form, it does not 'qualify' as abuse" (67).

Ms Keate raised numerous other concerns about various professors, the head, and the department more generally. The head, she said, had failed to deal "in context" with her "climate" concerns; a professor had shown a "dismissive and negative attitude" in respect to one of her papers; students were regularly stereotyped "on the basis of their performance during the first semester of a six-year doctoral program," and the department failed to recognize the problems in one of its subfields. In addition, one professor had "sexist, racist and conflict-

promoting" teaching methods (61–2). She concluded by saying that
she considered it her "civic duty to remain and to seek justice and
protection for myself and for other graduate students" (67–8). In a
later letter to the department head, she stated that she was "withhold-
ing proceeding with a Chilly Climate charge against the department
as a whole, pending developments in my program over the next
months" (62).

Responses from Named Faculty

As faculty were named in Keate's allegations and as the dean of FOGS
had not intervened with cautions to maintain confidentiality, the department head asked for responses from the named faculty. In the case of
professor H, whose grade was changed, a fair summary of the events
would have included his input. He said that Ms Keate had thanked
him in writing for "offering a great seminar," and he submitted a
complete copy of his handwritten criticism of her paper together with
her responses. It was his habit to keep copies of such material on file.
Of course, the reading of a critique is usually more painful for the
person to whom it is addressed than to others. I would characterize
his assessment as tough and critical, but not unfairly harsh. His
comments were extensive and detailed, indicating that he took her
intellectual work seriously. Responses from other named faculty similarly revealed different interpretations of events.

Racist Comments at Seminar

There was, finally, one accusation reported by McEwen about an
incident during a seminar in 1990. A "female PhD student of colour"
alleged that, during this event, "blatantly racist comments about blacks
and Africans were made in response to a woman of colour asking a
technologically specific question which had nothing to do with whether
anyone in the room was 'white' or 'black' or not. Alarmingly, not one
faculty member in the room, including the chair, responded, or indicated
that the speaker was out of order" (66, also noted in chap. 4). The
faculty member and the PhD student co-organizers of seminars for that
year were asked in 1994 to respond to this allegation. None of them
could recall such an event, though none had attended every seminar.

DECISION TO MOVE TO AN INQUIRY

The entire department at this point stood accused of a general failure
to support female graduate students, "women of colour," and persons

whose first language was not European; of stifling dissent and persistently treating students' complaints as untrue and unimportant; of failing to provide applicants with accurate information about departmental strengths and weaknesses; and of burying complaints against faculty or continuing to assume innocence in the face of what the students regarded as sufficient evidence to the contrary.

As these allegations indicate, there were many levels and multiple targets. The accused were required to maintain confidentiality throughout this process, and indeed they were often unaware of the charges against them or the names of their accusers, yet at least two of the students were on record as having sent specific allegations, with names, to individuals, newspapers, and other organizations external to the university.

It was increasingly evident that no resolution would be possible without a public inquiry and, in midsummer 1994, in my position as dean of arts I recommended to the department's faculty that they request an investigation. This they did. Later that summer Joan McEwen was appointed to conduct an inquiry, and ten months later she produced the Report.

CHAPTER FOUR

Demography and Discrimination

The initial complaint, the second memorandum, the actions of the dean of FoGS in the fall of 1993, and the McEwen Report all alleged or rested on the belief that there was a massive exodus of women from graduate programs in political science. The head of the department several times refuted the claim, but factual data on admissions and withdrawals, as well as on grades and awards, were ignored.

In a postmodern ideological climate it is fashionable to assert that science (often equated with anything quantitative) is not neutral; that it is male biased, that the way it poses questions and seeks answers predisposes its practitioners towards answers that are frequently inapplicable, irrelevant, and inappropriate to or downright biased against minority groups and women. As well, as McEwen reported, some of the participants in the affair regarded the attempts to ascertain the facts and to seek evidence as pigeon-holing information. What was required, said these critics, was a more holistic, gestalt approach to truth.

Statistical information and certain other kinds of data derived from what scientists would call objective studies tend to fall into this category of male-biased, pigeon-holing science. However, if one takes this position, one has to maintain it consistently. One cannot accept as valid the results of the graduate survey yet refuse to accept statistics on admission rates and grades by gender or minority group, or the student evaluations done in March 1994, as Ms McEwen did in her report. On this ground, it seems fair (a word from the modernist, not postmodernist, lexicon) to look at the full range of quantitative data.

First, I shall give the demographic data on faculty and students, and then the admissions, withdrawals, grades, and awards data for students in graduate classes. The 1994 graduate survey will be examined in some detail, and the annual student evaluations briefly noted. The final section of this chapter is free of numbers, though it is occasionally concerned with them; it reports on reviews of the department that were completed in the period between the first and second round of allegations.

DEMOGRAPHIC PROFILE: FACULTY

At the time of the initial allegations, the Department of Political Science had twenty-two full-time faculty members, three of whom were female; none was identifed as a member of a minority ethnic group. The majority of faculty were in their fifties or early sixties. A high proportion had obtained their final degrees in American universities. This demographic profile was fairly typical of social science departments in the 1990s. The student body changed more rapidly than the faculty because faculty were hired for the length of a normal working life, and these faculty members had been hired (as had many others in all disciplines at UBC) during the late 1960s and early 1970s when their disciplines were popular and universities were expanding rapidly. The hiring preferences at that time undoubtedly favoured men, but even if they had not done so, it would have been hard to find an alternative: there were few women or non-Caucasians in the recruitment pool who had a PhD. The rarity of Canadian PhD degrees also reflected the period of recruitment. In the social sciences, UBC itself only started up PhD programs in the late 1960s and early 1970s. There were not even many degree-granting institutions in Canada before then.

The Department of Political Science differed from other social science departments at the University of British Columbia in one respect: it decided early in its development that it would give no introductory undergraduate course at the first-year level. This reduced the need for additional faculty and also for numerous graduate teaching assistants. It was decided to restrict the number of students entering the major's program and to put resources into a very high quality honours program. Much of the faculty's collective energy had been devoted to these quality endeavours. The slow growth in faculty members, though largely a result of reduced funding, was in part a product of these decisions.

For several years in the 1980s, hiring had been frozen at UBC. When it was again permitted, the department added two women, thereby bringing the total to three by 1992. In the next couple of years, two more women (one of Asian descent) and one man (also of Asian descent) were employed. A few of the appointments were shared with other units, so full-time faculty numbers actually increased by only two in the decade 1985–95.[1] The new recruits were welcomed to the

Table 2
Department of Political Science, basic statistics, 1986/87 to 1994/95

	1986/87	1987/88	1988/89	1989/90	1990/91	1991/92 1 July 1991	1992/93 1 Jan. 1993	1993/94 7 Mar. 1994	1994/95 19 May 1995
FTE, faculty	21.00	21.00	22.00	22.00	22.50	22.50	23.00	23.50	23.50
FTE, U/G	395.00	378.00	395.00	396.50	390.70	376.50	338.70	340.60	296.20
S/F ratio, U/G	18.81	18.00	17.95	18.02	17.36	16.73	14.73	14.49	12.60
MA students (HC)	19.00	42.00	28.00	28.00	37.00	44.00	41.00	29.00	41.00
PhD students (HC)	11.00	17.00	14.00	16.00	15.00	22.00	27.00	30.00	37.00
S/F ratio, graduate	1.43	2.81	1.91	2.00	2.31	2.93	2.96	2.51	3.32

Source: Faculty of Arts comparative departmental statistics, compiled in July 1995 (from department profile information, UBC Budget and Planning Office)

FTE = full-time equivalent

FTE U/G = is based on course enrolment and normal credit load of 30. The FTE for a course is calculated by using the following methodology: (course enrolment × course credit value) ÷ 30

S/F = student faculty

HC = headcount

U/G = undergraduate

department. But although the atmosphere was hospitable, there were unavoidable differences between the older cohort of post-family males and the younger recruits, in lifestyles, interests, and levels of material wealth.

DEMOGRAPHIC PROFILE: GRADUATE STUDENTS

There were 66 graduate students in 1992, more than twice the number enrolled five years earlier; their numbers continued to increase until 1994/95. By 1992, two-thirds of these students were enrolled in the MA program; the proportion of female students in the program had steadily increased so that by this time the ratio was about 50:50. The PhD program, which had 11 students in 1986, had twice that number in 1992 and 37 students by 1994/95; the proportion of women in the PhD program had increased to about one-third by 1992. These proportions were not unusual in academic departments. Indeed, political science had more female graduate students than several other departments at UBC. The department also had about 350 "full-time equivalent" undergraduate students in majors and honours programs.[2]

UBC's Department of Political Science actively recruited non-Canadian students, so the student body was multicultural. At least fourteen national origins were noted by Ms McEwen.

Admissions and Withdrawals

Over its history, fewer women than men had entered the PhD program: 83 men to 26 women between 1970/71 and 1994/95; 27 men and 9 women over the five-year period from 1990/91 to 1994/95. However, there was a gradual increase in the number of women after 1980/81. Twenty-one of the 26 women entered the program between 1980/81 and 1994/95. The pattern is similar to that of other social science programs.

Of those enrolled in the PhD program since 1970/71, 15 men and 4 women had withdrawn. These withdrawals refer to voluntary abandonment of the program for any reason except medical leave or transfer to another university; they do not include involuntary withdrawals due to failed examinations. The proportions over the total period were almost the same (15 per cent of women, 18 per cent of men). In the period 1990/91 to 1994/95, one man and two women withdrew, too small a difference to support generalizations. Of the 1980–89 cohort, two women and one man who had entered in 1988/89 remained in the program in May 1995. These, together with the withdrawals for medical and transfer reasons, contributed to the low

Table 3
Statistics on admissions to Department of Political Science, by gender, 1990–1995[1]

	MA	PhD
APPLIED		
Male	334	168
Female	203 (38%)	68 (29%)
Total	537	236
ADMITTED		
Male	123	48
Female	86 (41%)	23 (32%)
Total	209	71
ENROLLED		
Male	51	31
Female	50 (50%)	12 (28%)
Total	101	43

[1] As compiled on 19 September 1995

Table 4
MA students: Enrolment and completion numbers by gender, 1980/81 to 1994/95[1]

	1980/81 to 1984/85	1985/86 to 1989/90	1990/91 to 1994/95
ENROLLED			
Male	31	53	43
Female	19	25	47
Total	50	78	90
COMPLETED			
Male	22	40	29
Female	11	19	28
Total	33	59	57
% OF ENROLLED WHO COMPLETED			
Male	70	75	67
Female	58	76	60
Total	66	76	63

[1] As compiled in September 1995

completion rate. The withdrawal rates for the department as a whole were not unusual for the humanities and social sciences in that same period.

In the MA program comparable data were available for the period 1980/81 to 1994/95.[3] In the whole period, 127 men and 91 women were enrolled. For the early period and up to the end of the 1980s, more men than women were enrolled. Equal numbers were enrolled

Table 5
PhD students: Admissions, completions, failures, and withdrawals, by gender, 1970/71 to 1994/95[1]

Year	Admissions		Completions		Comprehensives failures		Voluntary withdrawals		Other[2]	
	M	F	M	F	M	F	M	F	M	F
1970/71 to 1979/80	29	5	22	4	0	0	7	1	0	0
1980/81 to 1989/90	27	12	16	4	2	2	7	1	1[3]	2
1990/91 to 1994/95	27	9	n/a	n/a	1	1	1	2	0	1
Total	83[4]	26[4]	38[5]	8[5]	3	3	15	4	1	3

[1] As compiled on 30 May 1995
[2] "Other" includes medical leave and transfers to other universities or programs
[3] Did not complete thesis in time
[4] Percentage total admission by gender: 1970/71 to 1994/95, male 76, female 24
[5] Completion as a percentage of admissions by gender: 1970/71 to 1979/80, male 76, female 80; 1980/81 to 1989/90, male 59, female 33

in 1989/90, and from 1992/93 onward more women than men were enrolled.

Over the total period, 91 men and 58 women completed their MA degrees. Omitting the 12 students admitted in 1994/95 (who could not have completed by the time the data were compiled), the completion rate for men was 73.2 per cent and for women 70.1 per cent – not a significant difference. In the five-year period from 1990/91, 43 men and 47 women were enrolled in MA programs. Of these, 6 men and 5 women withdrew. Over the decade from 1984/85 to 1994/95, 21 men and 12 women withdrew. As can be seen, in numbers relative to totals, men withdrew more frequently than women.

Overall, then, the allegations about admissions and withdrawals are not borne out by the data.

On the other hand, there appear to be grounds for arguing that some parts of the PhD program were poorly handled. Instructions may not have been clear, and students may not have been adequately prepared. Faculty members acknowledged that there were weaknesses and had undertaken to overhaul the whole program even before the McEwen Report came out. The question for McEwen was whether the deficiencies differentially affected female students or non-Caucasian students, rather than whether there were weaknesses.

One of the students (possibly more, but it is impossible to tell from the way the allegations were set out) contended that essential preparatory information was differentially available by race. Since neither the department nor the university gathers statistics on race, one cannot test the allegation except inferentially by performance measures for persons identified by faculty members as visible minorities or by nationality. This is not a perfect measure, but it is the only one available.

The data show that three women and three men had failed comprehensives in the entire history of the PhD program beginning 1970/71 up to and including 1994/95. One of the women and none of the men in this group were identified as being members of ethnic minorities by a current graduate adviser who used nationality as a criterion and who consulted with the students' supervisors regarding visible ethnic minority status.

Withdrawal rates also were scrutinized by the adviser, using the same criteria. Fifteen men had withdrawn. Of all men identified as members of ethnic minorities, 20 per cent had withdrawn, compared with 17 per cent of others not so identified. The difference is not sufficient to substantiate a claim of discrimination by race for men. Of the four women who withdrew, none was identified as a member of an ethnic minority.

Over the period since 1970/71, of twenty-six female enrollees (including seven tentatively identified by faculty as members of ethnic minorities),[4] eight had successfully completed the degree (a rate of 47 per cent when current enrollees were excluded). Eight were still enrolled, four had withdrawn, two had transferred to other universities, one had died, and three had failed comprehensives. In the same period, of eighty-three male enrollees in the PhD program (of whom fifteen were tentatively identified as members of ethnic minorities), thirty-eight had successfully completed a degree (a completion rate of 68 per cent when current enrollees excluded). Twenty-six were still enrolled, fifteen had withdrawn, one had failed to complete by the deadline, and three had failed comprehensives.

These data do not support the view that women and female visible ethnic minorities withdrew or failed in disproportionate numbers, either in the recent past or over the history of the program. They do support the view that a lower proportion of women speedily completed the degree, though the pattern was not inconsistent with that of the university at large. To move beyond these data we need to know the reasons for progress rates, but no systematic investigation of such differences has been undertaken. It is possible that women more frequently take leaves of absence from the program: maternity leave and competing domestic responsibilities are accepted reasons for taking time out from studies. Women might also leave programs more frequently than men because of spousal relocation. These are both reasons related to gender, but they could not appropriately be attributed to sexism on the part of the university or the department.

While no study has been undertaken of differences in length of time taken to complete degrees, the department did undertake an informal study of the reasons for withdrawal from its graduate programs. The graduate adviser gave McEwen a list of all students who had left the PhD program in the period 1985/86 to 1993/94, citing the reasons when known.[5] The matter of interest to us is how many of these left for performance-related reasons. The list shows that four men and two women withdrew because of poor grades, another man failed to complete his thesis, one woman withdrew after failing one comprehensive (rather than undergoing a second one), and one male and two females failed comprehensives (mandatory withdrawals). Overall then, six men and five women left for academic reasons. (A second male failed comprehensives in 1994/95 but is not included in these data.)

In terms of the proportion of male and female students who left the PhD program during this period, this shows no differentiation by gender even though one more of the women proceeded as far as the comprehensives before withdrawing. However, in terms of ratios of their total numbers in the program, women more frequently left for performance-related reasons. Omitting those who had graduated or withdrawn before 1985/86, there were eighteen women who had enrolled in or after that academic year (including all still enrolled in 1995/96). Of these, five (or 27.7 per cent) failed or withdrew for academic reasons. By comparison, again excluding those who had already left the program in 1985/86, there were forty-three males enrolled during the same period. Of these, six (or 13.9 per cent) failed or withdrew for known academic reasons.

A profile was also provided for MA students. Concentrating again on performance-related reasons, the adviser recorded that three men and one woman had withdrawn because of poor grades, seven men and three women failed to complete course work, and four of each group had failed to complete a thesis. The totals are fourteen men and eight women who withdrew for academic reasons. Since in this period the proportions of men and women in the program were fairly even, the higher proportion of men who withdrew, and the higher proportion who failed to complete course work or who received poor grades, might indicate reverse discrimination (no one has suggested that!), or it might indicate a trend that the department should consider. Perhaps the Department of Political Science in the 1990s has been attracting more academically strong women to its MA program but fewer academically strong men.

It seems clear from the above data that as far as the withdrawal and failure rates are concerned in the MA and PhD programs, the argument about systemic racism and sexism is difficult to sustain. If there was either systemic or pervasive discrimination, it would show up in both MA and PhD programs (and in undergraduate courses too), but there are no grounds for concluding that it was a factor. However, there are grounds for worry about the PhD completion rates. Proportionately more women than men left for academic reasons, whether because they failed courses or comprehensives. One must beware of reaching for conclusions on the basis of five instances out of eighteen because the numbers are so small. Even so, a fair investigator would not want to lose sight of this information.

All of these data were accessible to the dean of FoGS and the investigator. In addition, Ms McEwen had the names of the students who had left the program, and she had detailed information on the current employment of PhD graduates when known. Several ex-students, both those who had left the program and those who had graduated, contacted her and gave interviews, and she contacted others. Yet the range of perspectives from these students is truncated in the report. Nowhere was it noted, for example, that since 1987, twenty PhD graduates had been hired by universities in Australia, Norway, the United States, and Canada. Among this number were four of the women who had graduated since 1987, and two of these women were members of visible minorities.

ACADEMIC STANDARDS

High female withdrawal rates constituted one of the persistent and inaccurate claims in the student allegations, and they were repeated in the McEwen Report, despite the availability of data showing that this was not the case. Another of the claims was discriminatory grading practices. Since this was also implied in the evaluations data in the graduate survey, this may be the appropriate place to scan some of the quantitative data on grades and nominations for academic awards.

Academic standards might be used by a dominant group as a blanket to justify behaviour motivated by ill will, rudeness, sexism, racism, or any other nastiness. However, universities are mandated to establish and sustain academic standards. If a department establishes an academic standard essential for passage of comprehensive examinations at the PhD level, then, provided the same standard is evenly and fairly applied, the matter is academic, not personal. The question for McEwen was whether there was a basis to the claims that racism and sexism influenced grades so that students who failed comprehensives

Table 6
Grade distribution in graduate courses, by gender, winter 1993/94[1]

	Women					Men				
	A	B	C	F		A	B	C	F	
Number	48	22	0	0	70	44	21	1	1	67
Per cent	69	31			100	66	31	1	1	99

[1] Grades for 1994/95 were not available when this table was constructed in September 1995

were really failing gender and race tests. She did not undertake any examination of the comprehensives, and she dismissed all empirical data provided by the department about the numbers who had passed and failed over several years. On the basis of this evidence, the claims could not be sustained.

Specifically, in the department as a whole, the percentage of PhD students receiving A grades between 1989/90 and 1993/94 did not differ systematically by gender. In three of these years a fractional percentage more As went to males than to females, but in two other years the opposite was the case. Since there were more men than women in the program, this would suggest that proportionately more women received A grades.

Secondly, a review of all graduate course grades for the winter session 1993/94 showed no significant gender difference. In proportions of each gender group, 69 per cent of women and 66 per cent of men received A grades; no women received C or F grades, but 2 per cent of men did.

DISTRIBUTION OF AWARDS

The PhD program of the period between 1987/88 and 1994/95 had about 33 men and 14 women (since a cohort of students does not move through the system all at once, numbers vary between start and finish dates.) Assuming equality of talent and allocation, we should note roughly the same ratio of nominations for university graduate fellowships, that is, about 70 per cent for men and 30 per cent for women. The data are available to test this, and they show that 71 students were nominated: 55 (77.4 per cent) male and 16 (22.5 per cent) female. Thus, the proportion of women nominated was below the expected level. The actual allocation of rewards was made by a committee under the dean of FoGS, and this committee awarded 49 PhD fellowships to the department, on a ratio of 37 (75 per cent) to men and 12 (25 per cent) to

Table 7
University graduate fellowships: Nominations and success rates by gender, 1988/89 to
1994/95, compared with enrolment of MA and PhD students in the Department of
Political Science[1]

	Male	Female	Total
MA STUDENTS			
No. of students enrolled	60.0	58.0	118.0
% of students enrolled	50.8	49.2	100.0
No. of nominations	18.0	27.0	45.0
% of nominations	40.0	60.0	100.0
Number successful	9.0	15.0	24.0
As % of successful	37.5	62.5	100.0
% of all enrollees in gender group	15.0	25.8	20.3
PhD STUDENTS			
No. of students enrolled[2]	37.0	14.0	51.0
% of students enrolled	72.5	27.5	100.0
No. of nominations	62.0	19.0	81.0
% of nominations	76.5	23.5	100.0
Number successful	41.0	13.0	54.0
As % of all successful	76.9	24.1	100.0

[1] Compiled in September 1995. Students may be nominated more than once in
  successive years, so total nominations over a six-year period would exceed the
  number enrolled at the PhD level. As a consequence, success rates for gender groups
  cannot be calculated.
[2] PhD enrolment numbers are approximations deduced from admission rates minus
  completions prior to 1988. They may be slightly inaccurate.

women. The external committee, then, slightly improved the distribution
in favour of women though the end result remained inequitable.

The distribution of university fellowships for MA students reversed
the inequities. For this period the numbers of men and women were
in fair balance in the MA program, so the expected distribution would
be about 50 per cent to men and the same to women. In fact the
department nominated 40 individuals, 16 (40 per cent) male and 24
(60 per cent) female. The external committee reduced both by about
half (8 men and 13 women) but did not substantially change the ratio.

The same pattern showed up in most of the data so far surveyed.
The gender imbalance at the PhD level was offset by a balanced
distribution at the MA level; the disproportion in exits and withdrawals
as a result of academic failings at the PhD level was offset by greater
retention and lower failure rates for women at the MA level; and the
higher proportion of nominations for men at the PhD level was offset
by a higher proportion of nominations for women at the MA level.
These data again suggest that there was a problem in the PhD program,

but to label this as pervasive sexism and racism was not appropriate as long as the opposite trends were apparent in the MA program. The same teachers instructed, graded, and nominated both groups of students.

GRADUATE STUDENT SURVEY CONDUCTED FEBRUARY 1994

The dean of FoGS, together with the Graduate Student Society and the Women Students' Office, sponsored a campus-wide survey of graduate student attitudes and opinions in February 1994. Final results for the whole campus were distributed in September 1995. Responses to selected sets of questions, showing percentages with breakdowns by discipline and gender, were given to Ms McEwen and others, including myself, in December 1994. Ms McEwen selectively reported the research data in the Report. Because the survey was conducted independently of her investigations, I shall discuss it here rather than in chapter 6 with the rest of the McEwen Report.

Of 69 students in political science to whom the questionnaire was sent, 36 responded: 20 men and 16 women (the men were evenly divided between MA and PhD programs; four of the women were in the PhD program). The response rate was thus 52 per cent, compared with 59 per cent for the campus as a whole. There is no explanation in the Report for the decision of the other 33 students in political science to leave the questionnaire unanswered.

Because of the low response rate and the timing of the survey (graduate students had by then submitted their second memorandum, and rumours of allegations were rife throughout the department), the survey's chief researcher wrote in his covering letter many months later: "I do not have sufficient information to comment on how representative the Political Science group is of all Political Science students registered in the spring of 1994."[6] The timing was unfortunate, but the chief researcher had no reason to be aware of what was happening in political science at the time of sending out the questionnaires. He may not have recognized the implications until the Report published the selected results of the survey. The survey was criticized for insufficient response rates, lack of sample representativeness, deductions based on cell frequencies too low for statistical inference, and leading questions. However, the chief researcher was cautious in his reading of the results, and he provided appropriate warnings to others about the limitations of the survey. He pointed out that the respondents were not a random sample and that statistical inferences were thus of dubious value.

The researcher provided McEwen with a summary of responses to 97 selected questions. She published the responses for 11 of these questions in her report. Readers were not informed of the selection criteria or that these were 11 out of 97 possible choices. All of the published response arrays showed the department in a poor light. The full range, however, indicated that the more factual the questions were, the less divergent political science students were from other social science students or UBC graduate students more generally. Some of their responses were more negative and some were more positive than the responses of other students. Men and women differed, but not always in ways one might expect after reading the Report.

The major differences were on questions about feelings. As quoted in the Report, the chief researcher noted that women in political science rated their experience more negatively than women in other social science departments. He said:

This is especially noticeable for the questions related to "disparaging remarks," "verbal abuse of students," "professor's use of inappropriate metaphors," and the "treatment of different cultures." Women in Political Science are much more likely to use words like "biased," "elite," "exclusive," "masculine," and "rejecting," in describing their department than are women in other Social Science departments. The descriptive words used by men in Political Science are less likely to differ in major ways from their counterparts in other Social Science departments. (18)

Supporting the argument that women in political science were less satisfied than other students were a number of items, including one about satisfaction with the UBC experience. On this, 44 per cent of women compared with 65 per cent of men in the department reported that they were very or moderately satisfied. More men than women expressed satisfaction with comprehensive examinations and evaluations. On a range of questions about feelings of worth, of being appreciated, of being isolated, of being in control of events affecting them, between 20 and 40 per cent of women respondents in the department (3–6 individuals) gave negative responses. A higher proportion of female respondents in political science than in other subjects gave these negative responses.

Other sets of questions contradicted the general argument that women were especially unhappy, or else the responses were less easily interpreted. For example, more women than men in political science reported that their supervisors provided specific suggestions or guidance on courses, and more said that their supervisors knew substantive areas in relevant discipline(s). The 63 per cent who said that their

Table 8
Graduate student survey: Percentage agreeing or strongly agreeing that the statement
best represents their current relationship with their graduate supervisor

Statement	Political science		Social sciences		UBC	
	Women	Men	Women	Men	Women	Men
When I wish to talk with my graduate supervisor, I need to make an appointment	44	35	57	42	50	36
My supervisor tends to break appointments	0	5	7	6	8	8
My supervisor and I meet regularly	56	45	37	39	44	55
We talk primarily about degree requirements	31	15	35	27	32	29
My supervisor takes too much credit for my work	0	0	3	2	3	6
I would like to spend more time with my supervisor	13	25	42	40	39	41
My supervisor is somewhat indifferent to what I do	19	5	21	15	19	16
My supervisor helps me solve intellectual problems	50	70	54	55	58	64
My graduate career was interrupted because my supervisor was absent for an extended period of time	6	5	8	5	6	5
My supervisor returns written work to me promptly	56	60	52	54	54	58
My thesis topic is closely tied to my supervisor's research	50	60	35	35	41	56
My supervisor provides me with intellectual stimulation	56	75	60	59	62	69
My life is excessively dominated by my supervisor	0	0	3	3	5	6
My supervisor encourages me to think independently	75	80	71	68	73	80
If I need feedback on a paper or piece of research, I feel comfortable talking to my supervisor	63	80	65	66	68	77
I find other faculty in the department/school easy to approach	38	65	57	57	60	65
My supervisor encourages me to publicly present my work	31	35	40	41	46	57
My supervisor helps me in developing my ideas	63	75	58	59	62	67
My supervisor undermines my self-confidence	13	10	10	8	12	10
My working relationship with my supervisor is exploitative	6	0	5	4	6	8

supervisors exhibited empathy, kindness, and understanding were a smaller proportion than the men who reported likewise (75 per cent), but these proportions were not out of line with those of respondents in other disciplines. Table 8 shows the response pattern for a long and complete list of questions about student relationships with graduate supervisors. None of these questions was shown in the McEwen Report. The reader can judge whether these distributions support any particular argument about women in political science.

A somewhat puzzling response pattern showed up on questions about competition: more political science students of both sexes than other social science or other graduate students said that the atmosphere in their courses was competitive. More women than men in political science perceived the competition, compared marks, and said they found competition destructive. Yet a much higher proportion of women and men in political science than in other subjects said that they preferred to work alone on research projects, and more of them also said they believed that competition produced better results.

If the research team had treated the respondents as a sample rather than as a universe with a low response rate, they would have examined the results in terms of means and would have performed statistical tests to determine the probability of obtaining the differences in responses between men and women by sheer chance. A printout of this kind was produced. There were only 4 out of 97 questions and one scaled item where the differences by sex within the political science group were statistically significant. For the social sciences as a whole, 14 questions elicited differences between men and women that were statistically significant, and for the university as whole, the number of questions in this group was 26.

University financial support was everywhere lower for magistral than for doctoral candidates, as shown in the final report on this survey, distributed in September 1995. After adjusting for all other factors, differences by degree level were most significant. However, the differences by sex for students in the MA programs were substantial. The reported average monthly winter term income for women in the survey was lower than for men in every master's program at UBC, and the lowest incomes were received by women in the humanities and social sciences. Differences by sex and disciplinary divisions were less marked at the doctoral level.[7]

These patterns were also evident for political science students. Women in political science reported less financial support than men, and fewer women than men reported receipt of support from university sources. The summary of self-reported funds provided in December 1994 lumped together PhD and MA students at the department level, and the majority of female respondents were in the MA program. Because further breakdowns might reveal identities (especially when there were only four female respondents who were PhD candidates), researchers would not normally undertake more detailed analysis at the level of a department. Women enrolled in political science who responded to the survey reported average monthly incomes of $725; other female respondents in social science master's programs reported average monthly incomes of $712. Men enrolled in political science who responded reported average monthly incomes of $1,135. Male respondents to the survey who were in master's programs in the social sciences earned $806 and in doctoral studies, $1,101; since half the respondents from political science were doctoral students, the difference for the respondents would be partially but not wholly explicable as a function of degree differences. Eighty per cent of men in the survey, compared with just under 44 per cent of the women, reported receipt of funds from UBC. Again, this would be partially attributable to degree differences and possibly to differences between full- and part-time situations, but there can be little doubt at the end of the day that women throughout the university, in the social sciences and humanities in particular, and in this department, received less funding than men from university sources.

Readers can make what they will of this information, but the point is that this survey was much more comprehensive and less comprehended than is suggested by the eleven selected questions included in the Report. It was also more problematic because of its low reponse rate and its timing. A cautious reader might conclude that about half of the sixteen female respondents were dissatisfied with their department and graduate experience and that, according to their own reports, slightly less than half had low self-esteem and low self-confidence. One would conclude with less hesitation that a majority of women who responded, whether they were in political science or other subjects, and especially if they were enrolled at the magistral level, received no or very little university funding. In this respect they were clearly given unequal treatment. Beyond that, one could not say very much with certainty.

FACULTY OF ARTS TEACHING EVALUATIONS, MARCH 1994

As dean of arts I had tried during 1993–94 to persuade all departments to use a common student evaluation questionnaire that included three questions pertaining to perceptions of racism, sexism, and general decency of relations with students. The Department of English objected strenuously, and someone circulated some rather vicious poster-style condemnations of the dean, leading a notoriously right-wing *Vancouver Sun* columnist to applaud the rebuke to a dean he perceived as a "politically correct" feminist. Yet one of the departments that enthusiastically adopted the questionnaire, including the three questions, was political science. Its members could see that having responses to those questions would be useful either as a warning of the need to change or as protection against further allegations. The first time the questionnaire was used throughout the department was in March 1994.

In all, more than 1,400 questionnaires were completed in political science courses, and the results were very favourable to faculty. According to the (computer-analysed) responses of these students, more than 50 per cent of whom were female, the instructors treated students with equal respect regardless of sex, culture, or other special characteristics; the instructors did not use language, examples, or stories that were demeaning either to women or to men; and they did not use language, examples, or stories that were demeaning to members of certain racial or cultural groups. The faculty members cited in the complaints by Ms Jones and those seemingly implicated in several other cases in the 1992 and 1993 memoranda or named in other correspondence, had positive scores, all within one decimal point on either side of the mean for the department as a whole.

DEPARTMENTAL REVIEWS, FALL 1992 AND SPRING 1993

Between the two student complaints to the dean of FoGS in 1992 and 1993, a departmental review had been undertaken. The review was not done in response to the complaints; reviews are regular components of university governance, and it was the turn of the Department of Political Science. Three external reviewers, all highly regarded in the discipline, each wrote a short report following a two-day site visit. These reports became components of a more detailed review conducted by an internal committee of peers, who were located in other departments or in other faculties of the university. Thus, in total there were four reviews.

The external reviews were supposed to be confidential to the committee, the dean of arts and the dean of FoGS, the vice-president, and the president. The dean of arts, who commissioned the reports, had promised confidentiality in order to encourage frankness.[8] However, the dean of FoGS later contacted the external reviewers and requested their permission to give the reports to the investigator. Those parts that McEwen chose to reproduce are now part of a very public record.

The internal committee review called the department "one of the strongest departments of political science in Canada" and observed that its reputation "rests not only on the stature of a few internationally known scholars, but also on the high standard of the faculty generally." Further, "the University can take pride in the department's academic standing and accomplishments." The committee recommended, however, that the department "continue to take steps to increase the proportion of women" and to increase the breadth of its teaching fields specifically in the areas of Asian studies, international political economy, and gender studies and feminist political theory. The low proportion of women and the imbalance was emphasized.

The department was encouraged to reconsider aspects of its organization, and to "rethink its PhD program" because "its standing does not appear to be entirely commensurate with the department's significant strengths." The program needed a more effective advisory and mentoring system, a more targeted approach towards recruiting graduate students, and more effective arrangement of courses, comprehensive examinations, and other practices. The committee noted that it had been prepared to meet with all who expressed a wish to meet with it, but only "several graduate students" and no undergraduates had attended meetings.

There were comments about collegiality that are relevant to our study. In any North American university, one can find departments that are fraught with internal hostilities. This one, however, had carefully nurtured goodwill and tolerance. As well, the timing of its expansion in the 1960s had given it a demographic structure such that a majority of members were of roughly the same age and had similar academic profiles and similar life experiences. The potential cost of the department's tolerance was acceptance of human characteristics that might better have been discouraged and avoidance of intellectual discourse. A more general cost of the collegiality was that individuals who did not fit the demographic and other patterns – the more junior faculty hired later, women, and persons with different academic backgrounds – might well have felt estranged. The potential costs were noted by the internal review team.

The internal summary included components from the external reports, though the adequacy of the inclusions was later questioned by some university officers because of the selected renditions in the McEwen Report. One external reviewer praised the department as a strong one, a leading department in the fields of Canadian politics, political behaviour, and international relations. This reviewer noted some problems, however, including a weakness in comparative politics (no full professors; not strong; poorly organized at the doctoral level).

In this field, said the reviewer, graduate students had complained to the dean of FoGS and in review interviews that the department misrepresented its strength in Asian politics in its brochures. (It should be noted here that two senior professors in this field had recently retired and had not been replaced because there was insufficient university funding for replacements at senior levels.)

The same reviewer said that a second problem was the underrepresentation of women on the faculty. This reviewer noted that the dean of FoGS had provided information on the complaints by graduate students of "sexism and racism" but that "this episode was not raised with me by anyone in the department, although a modest version of the students' complaints were discussed by the graduate students whom I interviewed." This reviewer continued:

As long as the faculty is so predominantly male, however, the potential for such problems remains. With all good-will, the Head reported to the [FoGS] Dean that, in order to improve graduate student morale more generally, it had been suggested at the Departmental retreat that faculty "engage in more 'aggressive' (sic) mentoring of new graduate students." The use of that language in that context is an indication of a culture which may well be a "chilly climate" for women.

The second external reviewer praised the department, noting several "truly outstanding scholars" and its "enviable reputation as a scholarly unit," but also noting that the recent retirement of senior scholars in Asian studies had reduced the strength of the comparative-Asian field. According to this reviewer, the department's small size was a problem, and it needed more people in international relations and other fields. In particular, it needed more women faculty members, and it needed people who could teach feminist perspectives. This reviewer said that female graduate students complained about the lack of interest and support for feminist approaches.

The third external reviewer also praised the department but said that it was "at some risk, unless careful choices are made about the three matters" discussed in the review: governance, hiring, and the graduate program. This review needs to be cited in some detail because it pinpointed the flip side of the department's special strengths. It said, for example: "One great area of strength of the Department ... is its mature faculty, which is research-oriented, productive, committed to undergraduate teaching, and proud of the Department. Ironically, however, it is these very qualities which make the necessary transition to the next decade somewhat treacherous."

It said, as did the other reviews, that the demographic structure of the department constituted a problem: too large a gap between the "collegial" older cohort and the very recent appointees, in intellectual interests, family situations, and other characteristics. It said that the department had for too long given authority to a head instead of decentralizing to committees. In the reviewer's opinion, the department needed to add to its curriculum offerings in international political economy, gender and feminist theory, and some other subjects. In addition it had to hire more women. In this connection the reviewer said:

The Department ... has had a reputation of note for its seeming reluctance to hire women, as well as for some incidents of anti-feminist and somewhat sexist intellectual behaviour in the past. Such a reputation is unfortunate because it discourages women from applying to UBC. Moreover, it means that women students are without role models and may have greater difficulty finding mentors. A department of the calibre of UBC can not continue to sustain such gender imbalance.

This third reviewer noted the exceptional quality of the under-graduate and particularly the honours programs. But the flip side was that less emphasis and attention were given to the graduate programs. The reviewer also noted that the department concentrated in its grad-uate program, "whether deliberately or by chance," on training non-Canadian students. Among the graduate students, said the reviewer, there was a high level of discontent, ranging from "matters of course content and requirements to sexual harassment." Further, the reviewer recommended that the organization of the graduate programs, from advertising and advising incoming students through to comprehensives, be redesigned. There were too many uncertainties and ambiguities in the process.

SOME CONCLUSIONS

The quantitative data on admissions and on completion and with-drawal rates did not substantiate the claims of discrimination on grounds of sex or race. A central allegation, that numerous female students had left the graduate program, was simply untrue. As well, there was no substance to the claim that men were given higher grades than women and that they received more awards. There were differ-ences between the MA and PhD student cohorts, with women receiving more awards at one level and fewer at the other, but this difference did not support a theory of gender discrimination.

There were problems in this department, however, and some of the dissatisfaction with the PhD program showed up in a survey of students. Unfortunately, only half of the current students responded, and the survey was done in the midst of the allegations to the dean of FOGS. Still, the department recognized that some students, and more women than men, were not happy in their midst. As well, the survey informed them that their PhD program was not well organized. The external reviews were extremely laudatory about the productivity and scholarly strengths of the faculty, the academic quality of the undergraduate program, and the collegial relations amongst faculty. But they warned the department that some graduate students were dissatisfied, that the PhD program was deficient in some respects, that there were too few women in faculty positions, and that there was a need for courses on feminist theory. These problems were acknowledged by department members, and they were working on changes while the McEwen inquiry was underway.

CHAPTER FIVE

The Inquiry

The McEwen Report was the culmination of a ten-month inquiry. The inquiry's terms of reference, the number and selection of interviewees, the conduct of interviews, and much else later became controversial in their own right. Although this controversy erupted after the Report was submitted, the investigation of course preceded its production, so I shall pause here to discuss the inquiry before giving details of the Report.

I remind the reader that I participated in these events and cannot be an unbiased observer. I was the one who thought we should have an external investigation because the problem seemed so intractable. I was in the administrative group that chose Ms McEwen and developed the terms of reference. The Department of Political Science was in my bailiwick (though the graduate students were in FOGS). For the errors that are now so glaringly apparent in the selection of the investigator and her terms of reference, I accept my share of the blame. But as I said at the start, this is not an exposé, and my contribution to either the ills or the goods of this affair is ultimately neither here nor there. What matters is that we learn from this affair and recognize both its procedural errors and its philosophical implications.

APPOINTMENT OF MS MCEWEN

I blush to admit it, but I honestly do not recall how or why the small committee that met to decide on procedures for an investigation of the political science case chose Vancouver lawyer Joan McEwen as a sole investigator. She had taken her law degree at UBC and was known to some members of the law faculty. She had recently conducted an investigation concerning an individual at another university and was said to be a specialist in human rights cases in academic settings. We started out looking for several persons but somehow concluded that one person could do the job more expeditiously, and the vice-president appointed her. She agreed to work with an advisory group consisting of two respected professors emeriti and two graduated students who would be appointed by the Graduate Student Society. We did not make consultation obligatory, and it turned out that Ms McEwen chose not to consult at all. She met only once with the professors and, as far as I know, never with the ex-students. I met her for the first time at our initial interview in September, so until then I knew of her only through others, and they reported nothing alarming.

The administrative committee consisted of a vice-president, three associate vice-presidents, two deans, and occasionally others from the president's office. An associate vice-president chaired the meetings, but all who were present had equal voice. It was midsummer 1994, and members were in and out as holidays interrupted meetings. The group stopped meeting once the investigation started in September 1994. No one anticipated that it would continue until mid-June 1995 at a cost of $246,364.

THE TERMS OF REFERENCE

The terms of reference were controversial even before they were completed in draft. We anticipated that accused and accusers would be named during the inquiry, since the accused ought to be informed of who their accusers were and the nature of the accusations; but we wanted to let the investigator use discretion about whether names would be used in the public report. We decided that while the investigator should inform us about specific wrongdoing, she should not be in a position to recommend disciplinary action against individuals. That would be the task of the deans, following receipt of the Report.

Our initial drafts reflected these expectations. However, when we consulted the Faculty Association's executive representatives (including the association's president), and representatives of the Graduate Student Society (including both the president and Ms Keate, one of the complainants), they demanded that names should not be disclosed at any stage of the investigation. They were supported in this view by the dean of FOGS. All these people made it clear that there would be no cooperation unless anonymity and confidentiality were guaranteed. In addition, the Graduate Student Society's representatives threatened non-cooperation because they held that they should have called for and determined the parameters of the investigation. After much discussion, and in spite of the judgment of the legal adviser and others that failure to disclose names could lead to a report that blamed innocent as well as guilty people, we bowed to the pressures from the two major external groups involved in the process. We did allow the investigator some room for discretion, however, and she could have named individuals had she felt it necessary and appropriate. After the investigation had started, two prominent faculty members in the department further urged McEwen to name no names, and students also continued to agitate for anonymity.

The administrative group that put together the terms of reference assumed that the inquiry would require interviews with each faculty member and each of the complaining students, as well as other students, and that it would result in a balanced report that would allow the administration to determine the course for the department. On these assumptions, they directed the investigator to

enquire into allegations that there is pervasive racism and sexism in the Department of Political Science, particularly in its treatment of graduate students, and to determine whether, or to what extent, there is any basis for the allegations; to review any actions taken by the University in response to the allegations; and to enquire into such further matters, if any, which arise out of the Enquiry; to advise the Deans on whether the response of the University has or has not been adequate; and to make general recommendations to the Deans on any measures or actions which should be taken; provided, however, that the recommendations shall not be made on punitive actions that might be taken with respect to specific individuals.

The process allowed the investigator wide latitude to obtain documents, request interviews, and meet with any interested persons; and it directed that the investigation "shall be conducted in a manner that is fair to all. In particular, individuals shall be informed of the details of any allegations that may have been made against them and be given the opportunity to respond." Further: "The Enquiry shall treat as confidential the identity of those who meet with it and the testimony given to it, provided however that the identity of individuals and the testimony may be revealed if in the opinion of the person conducting the Enquiry that is necessary for the purpose of the Enquiry or to ensure fairness to those affected by it." Finally, as part of the terms of reference, it was stated: "The report of the Enquiry shall be made public and shall be distributed to faculty and graduate students in the department." This was, again, a direct response to the concerns of the graduate students, who were convinced that otherwise the administration would bury a critical report.[1] Ironically, the dean of FOGS publicly rebuked me later for "insisting that the Report of the Enquiry be made public." It was the very students he defended who insisted on this, not me.

The terms were given to Ms McEwen before they were distributed to others. She was especially asked to comment on them, and she had the opportunity to request changes before the terms were published. But she indicated satisfaction with them. She subsequently expressed the opinion that "in terms of identifying individuals in the Report, the Terms of Reference gave me flexibility," and she said it was she who "ultimately determined that, in the context of a climate report, referring to individuals by name would be neither appropriate nor constructive. The concerns which have been raised are collective concerns against the institution of the University, aimed at accessing educational equity and precipitating change, not ascribing blame to particular individuals" (30–1).[2]

Judicial Status of the Inquiry

The terms of reference did not make it clear whether this was or was not a preliminary investigation. As I recall our discussions, the question never arose. We assumed that the investigator would present us with her findings and that the university would then determine how best to act on the analysis and evidence. We assumed that any proper investigation would naturally embody due process so we did not explicitly direct that this be done.

Ms McEwen herself defined the inquiry as a nonadjudicative process, which would suggest that she considered it a preliminary investigation. But in that case, the focus should have been on findings, without any recommendations for action. The findings would then have been considered either by the deans who commissioned it or by a separate body, a university committee perhaps, charged with making recommendations. There is thus ambiguity and inconsistency in the terms of reference as we set them out and in Ms McEwen's interpretation of them at the time and in her report.

Ms McEwen quoted Professor Hestor Lessard of the Faculty of Law at the University of Victoria to the effect that the best way to conduct discussions on systemic issues is to shy away from "findings of innocence or guilt with respect to particular individuals, departments, or areas" (71). Instead, one should focus on "structures, practices and attitudes," together with practical avenues for change. McEwen suggested that her work was "consistent with the focus." She explained:

Because I am not involved in an adjudicative process, each allegation is not being presented because it has been proven to be "true" but, rather, because it represents part of an overall picture which the students say is interfering with their working and learning environment. In other words, just because a student says that she has experienced racism and/or sexism does not mean that discrimination has been proven, as a matter of fact, to have occurred. However, the fact that the behaviours are being experienced as "racism" and "sexism" as broadly as alleged is, at the very least, some evidence that a climate which is "chilly" for white females and people of colour may exist.[3]

It is the students' assertion that such a chilly climate in fact exists that signals a call for the development of "practical and positive strategies for change." (71–2)

In reference to her finding that there existed a basis for the allegations, she stated:

This in no way suggests that one or more faculty members are guilty of opprobrious misconduct. Rather, that finding represents my professional judgment that various systems, structures, individual attitudes and practices within the department may be creating barriers to full participation by white female students and the students of colour. It is hoped that, once the sources for the potential creation of those barriers have been identified, then the process of eradicating them may begin. (72)

Definitional Hurdles

The administrative group did not define certain crucial terms. One of these was "systemic discrimination." It refers to actions within an organizational framework that inadvertently disadvantage particular groups (for example, scheduling exams at times that conflict with the religious observances of a minority group, or scheduling classes at an hour that inhibits access by persons responsible for the care of young children). There is no implication that systemic discrimination is intentionally harmful. If one concludes that the system has given rise to inadvertent and unintentional discrimination against women or minority groups, the way to solve the problem is by developing processes that will eliminate the discrimination. One does not solve the problem by pointing fingers or charging people with sinful behaviour. The recommendations notwithstanding, McEwen agreed with this approach to systemic discrimination:

"Intention" is not a necessary component of either adverse effect or systemic discrimination. Rather the law focuses on the harmful effects caused by these forms of discriminatory behaviour. Secondly, recognition of the systemic dimensions of discrimination has shifted the emphasis from looking at the impact of discrimination on a particular individual, to the effect of that discrimination on the affected group as a whole. (72)

Another crucial term was "pervasive discrimination." This seems to have no legal meaning, and neither the terms of reference nor McEwen provided enlightenment. "Pervade" is defined by *The Concise Oxford Dictionary* as "spread through, permeate, saturate," so one might assume that the phrase refers to a state in which discrimination is so frequent, so unrelenting, that everyone and everything is affected by it. But even with such a definition in hand, one is left puzzling whether various actions alone or in combination amount to discrimination, let alone pervasive discrimination. For example, is the use of a word, phrase, metaphor, or example that offends a particular group in and of itself evidence of racism or sexism? McEwen argued that the intention of the speaker was irrelevant and that perception was what ultimately mattered. If this approach were to be adopted, there would be no definition at all; any statement or event could be labelled racist or sexist – in which case, pervasive racism and sexism would exist by fiat.

The group that created the terms of reference treated the words "systemic" and "pervasive" as interchangeable. McEwen treated "systemic" as a subset of "pervasive," though in practice throughout the Report she did not maintain the distinction. In her lexicon, the other component of "pervasive" is "direct discrimination," whereby an individual practises discrimination or harassment against another individual or group. The matter was elucidated in her text under the heading "allegations of pervasive racism and sexism":

What forms of discrimination are alleged in this case? The students point to two different kinds of discrimination, namely (1) those "direct" forms of discrimination which include such individual forms of harassment (intentional or otherwise) as telling crude jokes, engaging in inappropriate socializing with students, non-verbal harassment (such as staring at female students as they walk by) and, primarily (2) those "systemic" forms of discrimination that are "system(s)-based," and adversely impact on disadvantaged groups. (21)

The term "sexism" did not pose any problems. It may be defined as behaviour or institutional and cultural patterns that reduce access, opportunity, or evaluation of an individual or group on the basis of sex.[4] In this definition sex is a biological or physical characteristic, and it is assumed that there are two identifiable sexes though there may be several sexual orientations. Gender refers to the cultural identity associated with sex, including the effects of sexism over history.

Although a definition of racism could parallel that of sexism ("behaviour ... on the basis of race," as given in chapter 1), in fact the term "racism" is problematic. Race is generally used in an imprecise way to refer to clusters of people whose physical characteristics are similar – skin colour, blood types, hair characteristics, facial features, and anatomical features being the most prominent measures of similarity and difference. These similarities are assumed to derive from a shared gene pool. The *Oxford Illustrated Dictionary* defines race as a "group of persons ... connected by common descent" ... "a distinct ethnical stock" ... "any great division of living creatures." Racism is the "theory that fundamental characteristics of race are preserved by an unchanging tradition."[5] A more precise biological definition is not of much use since, with the massive mixing of peoples of all gene pools, the human population is not divided into groups demarcated by distinctive physical characteristics. The term "race" is thus not very helpful, and its extension, "racism," is somewhat ambiguous.

"Ethnicity" refers more generally to cultural characteristics, though it is sometimes used as a synonym for "race" or in conjunction with "race." Thus, one's ethnic roots might be "Afro-American" or "Ukrainian." Neither of these groups constitutes a distinctive physiological gene pool, but they may be distinguished from one another by reference to combinations of physiological and cultural attributes. What does not make sense is a bifurcation of the population into groups defined by a single physical attribute, such as skin colour.

Muddy definitions are a problem in an inquiry of this kind. The task we set McEwen was either far too large or foolish, but the fault did not lie only with those of us who wrote the terms of reference; it also lay with Ms McEwen, who agreed to the terms. In using the words "systemic" and "pervasive" within the terms of reference, we were caught up in the language of the accusers. They used these terms, and we directed McEwen to see whether there was "a basis" for their allegations, not at the time appreciating that we were directing her to detect something that was undefined and extremely ambiguous.

I do not recall why we ignored the problems with the term "racism," and it belatedly strikes me as odd, because my training as a sociologist has made me very uncomfortable with such imprecise words to describe very precise and extremely serious forms of behaviour. Curiously, other social scientists during the debate were equally dull in their recognition levels. None, to my knowledge, ever publicly acknowledged that the term was problematic, and some of them fell into the same trap as the academics who had not studied history or anthropology: they, too, divided the world into "whites" and "people of colour."

Perceptions as Facts

As will be evident by this point, Ms McEwen took the position that perceptions are the equivalent of facts when trying to assess the presence or absence of pervasive sexism and racism. Although the word "perception" did apparently once mean "recognized as something that is true," it is used in contemporary English to mean "sensed" or "saw," with no necessary implication of truth attached to the sense or sight; but perhaps we are now revisiting historical usage. The definition is not trivial, because there were many claims in the Report that were essentially no more than "perceptions" or "feelings" – for instance, when someone took offence but the offender was neither intending to offend nor aware of the perception.

McEwen argued that different people had different "thresholds" in their experience of racism. Observers and judges had to pay attention to those who were more sensitive, even if other people made no similar complaints. Ms McEwen argued that if one person believed herself to be abused or harassed, that was what mattered, not whether these practices were widespread and affected all.

CRITICISMS OF THE TERMS OF REFERENCE

Criticism of the Report was swift in coming and was trenchant on all counts. Singled out for much of the criticism were the terms of reference. Both supporters and opponents of the action taken by the president acknowledged the failure of the terms of reference to give adequate direction to the investigator for the conduct of a fair and balanced inquiry. I report here only on the more prominent examples.

Criticism from CAUT and the B.C. Civil Liberties Association

The Canadian Association of University Teachers was among the heavyweight critics. In a special report published in midsummer 1995, it offered these opinions:

Investigations are, and can only be, a preliminary step in the process of dealing with the these types of complaints. They are intended to place before the appropriate administrators the information necessary for them to make a decision as to whether or not there are reasonable grounds for further action. These preliminary investigations are not a substitute for an adjudicative process ...

In the particular case of UBC, then, it was not unreasonable for the administration of UBC to appoint Ms. McEwen to investigate the various charges and allegations within the Political Science Department. The mistake made by the administration was to treat this report as though it were a judicial decision, and to issue it to the world as though it was the last word rather than the first word on this affair. Furthermore, the administration decided to suspend the intake of students into the graduate program in Political Science without verifying Ms. McEwen's allegations.

The B.C. Civil Liberties Association took issue with the term "basis for" and said in a lengthy critique that McEwen

was not commissioned to determine whether the students' allegations are true, but only whether there was a basis for them. It is not stated in the mandate or the Report how the term "basis" was to be understood. It is therefore difficult to say with any precision what the test was that she was applying. From the conclusions one can surmise that Ms. McEwen interpreted her mandate as being: to determine whether the incidents reported by the students (if true) would support the broader allegations; and to determine whether there was some evidence for their truth (such as, they were not patently unbelievable and they were not inconsistent with known facts). In short, what she was asked for was the sort of evidence which would prompt a human rights body to accept a complaint for further investigation.[6]

The association blamed the university for setting such terms, but it also blamed Ms McEwen, "since it was she who interpreted her mandate."

The Advocate

Another heavy hitter was the *Advocate*, the journal of the Law Society of British Columbia.[7] About the terms of reference it noted that the phrase "whether, or to what extent, there is any basis for the allegations" was weak; it implied that the interpretation was left to the inquiry, which "interpreted its terms of reference very narrowly." Further, said the *Advocate*,

The Inquiry's approach to its investigative and fact-finding function appears to us to be misconceived. How could the University's attempts to address concerns about "pervasive racism and sexism" ... be assessed, and more importantly, how could "general recommendations" concerning remedial action to be taken by the University in future be made, when the Inquiry limited itself to answering only the threshold question of whether "the complaints raise a genuine issue for determination"?

The problem of whether the university intended the inquiry to follow a format similar to judicial inquiries was considered, and the *Advocate* concluded that giving the assignment to a lawyer suggested that it did expect procedures consistent with due process. It noted that notwithstanding that choice, "We have seen that the Inquiry quite self-consciously and expressly *was not* a quasi-judicial investigation, employing the usual battery of procedural safeguards that are often compendiously referred to under the rubric of 'due process.'" The *Advocate* then asked, just what was the inquiry's approach to the gathering of information and finding of fact. And it answered, "It is quite succinctly, and we think chillingly, described at pages 71–72 of the Report." In particular, the *Advocate* noted Ms McEwen's conclusion (quoted in full earlier in this chapter) that it was not "truth" that needed to be presented but "an overall picture."

Natural Justice and Preliminary Investigations

Natural justice, a term used in Canadian law much in the way that "due process" is used in the United States, requires that accused persons know what precisely is alleged and by whom, and that they have the right of rebuttal and a fair defence. One normally expects an investigation to look at evidence and not treat accusations as if they were sufficient to prove a case. Whether due process in this sense is required of a preliminary investigation turned out to be one of the issues in this case, together with the issue of whether this was in fact a preliminary investigation.

There were lawyers involved at a later stage who said that subjudicial inquiries such as this were not obliged to observe the normal requirement for natural justice, and that due process was served if the reporter merely announced a verdict without even giving reasons. The dean of FoGS asserted in his statement to the Graduate Council in October (see chapter 7) that the process used by McEwen was "consistent with administrative law governing enquiries where individual respondents are not being investigated."

A contrary view was expressed by John Sanderson, a Vancouver lawyer recognized as an authority on harassment procedures. As quoted in the *Globe and Mail*, he found the McEwen method unusual:

"It doesn't follow due process or allow representation or allow people to defend themselves. People have to have some confidence that the process is fair to everybody involved, which this wasn't."[8] His view was shared by the editors of the *Advocate*, as noted above.

Thomas Berger

Among the numerous critics of the terms of reference was a prominent member of the Board of Governors, the Honourable Thomas Berger. He argued against the president's disciplinary action during the Board meeting in July (immediately following receipt of the Report) and again at the next meeting of the board in early October. Failing on both occasions to move the president, though in the meantime the public furore over the Report had continued to mount, he submitted his resignation on 12 October – one week before the senate meeting at which the whole issue was to be debated. His resignation was kept a secret until 8 November.

Berger said in his letter of resignation that he felt strongly "that the University acted hastily and unwisely in its response to the McEwen Report ... The Report, not least because of the mandate Ms. McEwen was given, was flawed. The University, in its response to the Report, failed to observe the principle of due process." He concluded: "I do not want to be understood as joining the bandwagon of those denouncing 'political correctness.' Too often this is simply a label used to turn aside legitimate concerns. But there is a right way and a wrong way to inquire into such concerns. We chose the wrong way, and we have yet to acknowledge it."

CONDUCT OF THE INQUIRY

Flawed though the terms may have been, a far more serious matter was the conduct of the inquiry. Complaints were numerous about the investigator's dismissal of input that was contrary to her conclusions. Before dealing with the complaints on this score, we should consider the number and characteristics of those interviewed.

Numbers Interviewed

According to her published record, Ms McEwen conducted 225 interviews with approximately 100 past and present students, faculty, administrators, and others, both internal and external to the university. She said she interviewed 33 current graduate students of 76 enrolled in the program; 35 former graduate students (no further specification regarding selection processes, years when study undertaken, et cetera); and 21 undergraduate students (no further specification regarding selection processes, nor why undergraduates were interviewed, since the terms of reference and the issues were related to graduate students).

By adding together the 33 current and 35 former graduate students, the investigator created a list of 21 who were "positive" and 47 who "raised structural and/or systemic problems." Of 33 in the current program, she labelled 7 as "positive" and 26 as "negative" in their views of the department. Of all current enrollees 19 out of 36 PhD students and 14 out of 40 MA students were interviewed; in both cases, a majority of interviewees were said to be female. Ms McEwen also designated individuals by the terms "white" and "women of colour." She identified one or more students as "Jewish," though no others were identified by religious affiliation.

In addition to interviewing faculty in the department, administrators, and graduate and undergraduate students and ex-students, Ms McEwen requested interviews with faculty members and students of non-European descent outside the department insofar as she was able to identify them (presumably, with the help of graduate students or faculty members). She also talked by phone with persons living on other continents, whom she contacted or who contacted her.

Number of Complainants

It may be that the diverse complaints reported by McEwen were made by all 33 current and 35 former graduate students plus 21 undergraduates, or by this number minus the 21 graduates and 9 undergraduates whom she categorized as "totally or almost totally positive." The problem is that many of the complaints were identical to those made in the initial and second memoranda or in the public complaints lodged by Jones and Keate. These were spread through the Report, and while the determined reader might recognize the same "mature white female" or "Jewish MA female" or "woman of colour" from time to time, general readers would miss the designations; further, even these designations were sometimes absent.

The result is that readers do not know whether the same complaints were made by many different voices or by few. Nor is their capacity for judging this report assisted by phrases such as "many students" or "some students" in connection with complaints. One of the professors in the department offered the opinion that over half of the complaints cited in the Report were attributable to no more than eight graduate students. Much later in the history, twenty-nine graduate students made their objections to the suspension public, and Lesley Krueger said in a *Globe and Mail* column what increasing numbers of students were then declaring: that the complainants numbered between five and seven. Since even in the first two memoranda no more than fourteen professors were ever alleged to have been guilty, Krueger mused, "the nation is riveted by a debate that centres on half a dozen students fighting a dozen or so professors."[9]

The Prevalence of Undergraduate Opinions

Although the inquiry was supposed to focus on graduate students, many of the reported complaints were from the twelve (self-selected) undergraduates whom McEwen categorized as negative. Four (possibly five) of six instances of what McEwen labelled "sexist or racist individual faculty/student interactions" were about undergraduates (85–6). Two of six instances of "inappropriate socializing" cited in the Report were about undergraduates, and one was about a potential applicant to graduate studies (91). Yet independent student evaluations done at the conclusion of classes (and reported in the previous chapter) were extremely favourable, and these came from more than 1,400 students. The reader might ask, Were there insufficient instances to report about graduate students? Did they not come forward with similar claims? If the twelve complainants actually represented undergraduates, then the university should have taken action to forestall undergraduate programs rather than only graduate programs.

Another interpretation is that some professors whose behaviour was less than ideal taught only at the undergraduate level. But if their behaviour was so crass that it deserved recognition in so many instances, would it not have made sense to make it clear that this was the case, rather than lumping together the instances claimed by an entirely self-selected and very small sample of undergraduates with the somewhat larger though still self-selected sample of graduates?

Omission of Student Voices

To say that the Report is lacking in balance is an understatement. It omits student opinions that failed to substantiate the allegations; faculty responses to allegations are virtually ignored, and there is seldom any discussion of the context of the charges. In defence of this approach, one might perhaps argue that the voices of the complainants had not been heard, that they had not had a fair reception in the past, so now it was their turn. This may be so, or it may not. On the basis of the Report, we have the complainants' claim that they had not been heard through normal channels, and we have the department's rebuttal that these students had never expressed their complaints in terms of sexism or racism; indeed, that they had not expressed most of the complaints at all before talking to the dean of FOGS. Since there was no serious investigation of the history, we have two conflicting memories of what happened. McEwen chose the first, but the criteria for her choice are not clear to readers. In any case, would it justify omitting much of the evidence?

A student who had obtained her BA in political science and had been recommended for a Rhodes Scholarship by the department wrote to Ms McEwen in January 1995 saying that she had taken courses from many members of the faculty and that her experience was very positive. She spoke in glowing terms of the openness to criticism and debate, the excellent teaching, and the encouragement of critical thought. Further, she said that feminism was respected and was included in the curriculum. She offered to discuss the issues. But as she pointed out in a later letter to the president, McEwen never contacted her.

Similarly, a female PhD graduate of the department wrote to the president (the letter was later widely distributed) to express her distress that the Report appeared to represent female graduate students yet neither incorporated nor acknowledged the positive experiences expressed by many who had met with Ms McEwen. She said in part:

I am personally offended that I met with Ms. McEwen and gave evidence in good faith on the assumption that the proceedings would adhere to the principles of natural justice and the doctrine of fairness. The selective presentation of evidence and the failure to disclose evidence that might raise doubts as to the veracity of many of the complaints is unconscionable. I am outraged to discover that I have participated in a process that has ignored fundamental principles of justice and damaged the reputations of decent and honourable people. It is of profound concern that a report replete with such deficiencies is being accorded legitimacy by the University.[10]

After the Report appeared, a male doctoral student in the department also wrote to the president stating his concern over the process of the inquiry. He expressed sympathy for any student who experienced genuine discrimination, but said he had told McEwen that he did not believe department issues included sexism and racism amongst faculty. He informed the president that although he had described personal experiences that directly contradicted allegations in the Report and although he had called into question the integrity of one of the complainants regarding particular allegations, his views had not been noted in the Report in any way. He said his views and those of others who failed to support McEwen's bias had been deliberately marginalized. Further, he alleged that during their interview, McEwen had named another student and that other students also had experienced an inquiry that was "gossipy and tabloidish." He concluded that a well-organized group had distorted reality and that the administration and media had accepted this.[11]

In a letter of 8 August 1995, fifteen individuals, including current graduate students and recent graduates of both sexes and of several ethnic derivations, wrote to the president and others stating their wish to register their "extreme consternation." They said: "Many of the undersigned actively involved themselves in the enquiry, attempting to correct the scandalous and unjustified allegations of pervasive racism and sexism. However, our views, personal observations, and corroborating testimony, have been systematically expunged from the Report, presenting a highly distorted account of graduate student attitudes in the department." These students were joined by fourteen others in a petition that was presented shortly before the senate meeting in October (detailed in chapter 7). Again, they said that the Report did not represent them.

Staff Who Failed to Complain

According to McEwen, faculty members harassed the staff (three secretaries). This was the same allegation that had been made by the aggrieved students to the dean of FoGS in June 1992. The staff objected to the allegation as restated by McEwen, and on 28 June 1995 they wrote to the vice-president saying so. They described themselves as three women, two of whom were minority group members. All had worked in the department for a long time. They said they had voluntarily met with McEwen and had informed her that they had never been harassed by any faculty member. The vice-president did not offer a public statement to rebut the allegation.

Later, the chair of the women's committee of their union's local wrote to the president outlining the plight she imagined these secretaries were suffering. This caused the secretaries to write back, expressing their surprise at her depiction of their situation. They assured her that they did not face "the injustices of harassment and discrimination." as she had claimed. In fact, they said, "There are no issues of harassment and discrimination that the Administration needs to address as far as faculty-staff relations in the Department of Political Science is concerned."

The Interview Technique

Complaints from faculty who were interviewed were quietly expressed in the early stages; they became more vocal and angry as time went by. I myself was interviewed on four occasions, during which I was asked questions of the traditional "Have you stopped beating your spouse?" variety. I was also subjected to the interviewer's seemingly unstoppable gossip. Did I know that so-and-so had once been married to that person? What did I think of X's new marriage or of Y's comment on Z? I wrote down what I had heard in the second interview and then asked for a third one, at which I put my rendering of the previous meeting before the interviewer. She disclaimed ownership. Yet much of the gossip I had heard in that second meeting turned up in one form or another in the Report.

It was clear enough from day one that Ms McEwen regarded faculty members as guilty. She spoke several times about the problem of so many being male and "white." That in itself seemed to be sufficient proof for her of their guilt. When I objected, she told me that white middle-class women, especially successful women, could not possibly comprehend sexism and racism. I was deeply shocked by the implications of this and was even more shocked when I heard from others that she had made similar comments to them. In one case, she dismissed a South Asian woman who refused to concede that racism was endemic on the campus. The woman said she was made to feel that she was the equivalent of an Uncle Tom.

Finally, during my fourth interview, I refused to tolerate Ms McEwen's hectoring tone and innuendo style of interviewing any further. I walked out. However, faculty members in political science did not feel free to walk out, and they put up with hours of interrogation that many have since described as bullying. They told me that McEwen implied their guilt and invited their connivance in pointing the finger at others. She refused to listen to anything they said that did not support her beliefs, and she belittled them throughout the interviews.

Two weeks before the Report came out, four senior members of the Department of Political Science wrote to me of their concerns. They had waited with their letter so that it could not be interpreted as an attempt to alter the character of the inquiry or influence it, "but simply to put our position on the record." They said that the inquiry had failed to put the experience of graduate students into appropriate academic context. They noted that it had failed to "distinguish between specific complaints about individuals, for which there are standing university grievance procedures, and the issue of allegations of pervasive racism and sexism"; also that it had failed to give faculty members any clear sense of what pervasive racism and sexism might be so that they could address it. They said there was no clear indication of what would constitute evidence. Further, the inquiry had veered into a range of issues beyond its mandate:

Faculty have been asked, in interviews that stretched over hours, for their opinions on a vast range of issues peripheral to the inquiry: who would make a good department Head; how the curriculum should be ordered; models of thesis supervision; where faculty did their graduate work; the merits of the Ivy League; whether undergraduates are penalized for writing too much; the supposed existence of "anglophobia" in the Department; whether graduates of the department or spouses of faculty members should be considered for faculty positions ... As a result, the core issues have been neglected, the inquiry has been extended far longer than necessary, and the work of students and faculty has been seriously disrupted ...

Individuals being interviewed are rarely given written or even oral advance notice of what allegations will be examined or what matters will be discussed. Often faculty members have been baited in a way designed to encourage them to respond to unattributed comments about colleagues. This has been distasteful and counter-productive. These procedures are simply inappropriate and, we would hope, unacceptable.[12]

Another faculty member decided to state publicly his experiences of interviews. In a letter to the dean of FoGS, which was widely circulated before the October meeting of the university senate, Dr Kal Holsti wrote:

During my interview with Ms. McEwen (January 7, 1995), I asked her how she was dealing with the numerous submissions from past and present graduate students that challenged the allegation of "pervasive racism and sexism" in the Department of Political Science. She replied that this evidence was "of no consequence because it comes mostly from white, middle class women." I was so shocked by this statement that immediately upon leaving the interview room I wrote down her words. It is more than just curious that a person with this mind-set should conduct an inquiry into racism and sexism.

Ms. McEwen was given the addresses and telephone numbers of numerous former graduate students, including those who could testify first hand about gender and race problems, and asked to contact them to get their response to the allegations. She failed to contact these persons. She did speak with our first PhD student, a Guyanan, but commented that his evidence was "of no interest" because it failed to lend support to the allegation of "pervasive" racism and sexism in the Department ...

Ms. McEwen claims to have protected the anonymity of those who made allegations. But in her zeal to classify everyone by age, race, gender, and even religion, it is not difficult to identify the sources of complaints. What is remarkable is that about one-half of the allegations came from less than 8 individuals ...

Ms. McEwen's interrogation methods were unprofessional. She gossiped about other people during my "interview," inquired into the marital lives of faculty, and condemned actions of the latter that are neither illegal nor inconsistent with University policy. Most important, despite her refusal to use procedures of due process, she consistently threatened to identify by name the targets of allegations, thus forcing some in the Department to hire legal counsel.

In response to the above, one might argue that faculty were on the spot and could be expected to defend themselves. However, it is more difficult to dismiss input from graduate students who say they were interviewed but "sytematically expunged" from the record.

Characterization of the Department Head and Other Faculty Members

Apart from the substance of the allegations (which will be considered in the next chapter) and the omission of input from both students and staff who spoke well of the department, there was a very serious problem of bias in the reporting of the department's actions to correct problems and of the department head's behaviour and statements.

The head was treated with contempt throughout the Report. When he defended his faculty, he was viewed as failing to concern himself with the plight of graduate students. He disputed information that he regarded as untrue, and the truth was not tested; instead, his statement was treated as an obvious cover-up. When he produced statistical evidence that contradicted the claims made by students, the investigator either ignored the evidence or treated it as of no importance. When he expressed his frustration with the claims, he was depicted as irrational. The data he produced were not investigated, though the Budget and Planning Office should have been able to provide "objective" information if there was any doubt about departmental data. He was labelled "obstructionist" when he disputed claims, and the responses he generated from accused faculty were either not reported or were reported in such a manner that the reader could not connect the answers to the allegations.

As McEwen herself noted, she did not think it necessary to provide a full and fair hearing to faculty. In fact, the faculty responses to her charges were relegated to a short appendix, where they were reported as two- or three-line statements and were unconnected to the charges; they were thus virtually unintelligible, even when correctly reported.

McEwen's Rationale for Marginalizing Faculty Responses

By way of explaining her failure to give the faculty equal space in the Report, Ms McEwen stated: "Again because I have not been charged with the task of making juridical findings of fact, I do not propose to recount in detail, on an incident-by-incident basis, either the specific faculty responses to allegations of direct discrimination, or their responses to allegations of systemic discrimination. I will, however, include in the Report the broad categories of faculty response (See also Appendix B in this regard)" (72).

Finally, Ms McEwen gave no explanation of why she excluded most of the information and comments given by students and others that did not substantiate the allegations.

CHAPTER SIX

The Report

Ms McEwen concluded that there was a basis for the allegations against the Department of Political Science. Her conclusion rested on several inputs: (i) the two memoranda, which were quoted liberally in the McEwen Report; (ii) the dean of FOGS's contribution; (iii) the external reports; (iv) the graduate student survey; (v) her perception of the "white male culture" of the department; (vi) curriculum issues; (vii) several particular incidents, including the Jones case and graffiti in the Honours Reading Room; (viii) her evaluation of the steps taken by the department to address the complaints; and (ix) the sheer bulk of specific allegations, some of them of the "direct" and some of the "systemic" variety (not distinguished in the Report).

McEwen opened the Report with a summary review of the two memoranda and the student concerns. I will describe this review section but otherwise will concentrate on inputs (v) to (ix). Most of this will be rendered in McEwen's words and format, without editorial commentary. My analysis of the substance of the Report will be given in chapter 8, though in the present chapter I have inserted a few notes in which I comment on procedures and other aspects of the text.

SUMMARY OF STUDENT CONCERNS

Nine areas of ongoing concern were identified by McEwen (7–10):

1 Academic supervision: a lack of consistency and norms for supervisory duties, conduct of comprehensives, assignments, and grades.
2 Curriculum: inconsistencies between Graduate Handbook listings of specializations and actual capacities of faculty; a lack of pluralism in the curriculum, and exclusionary attitudes towards feminist and gender studies.

3 Sexual discrimination and bias: "patterns of exclusionary and marginalizing behaviour," including less time spent consulting and less
intellectual engagement with women students; absence of female
writers or feminist theory in the curriculum; and "photographs are
requested of applicants to the graduate program."

4 The second student memorandum on racism. Part of this was quoted
in chapter 1, notably the section beginning, "The first symptom of
racism is to deny that it exists." Another section of the same lengthy
statement began, "Nothing less than zero tolerance of racism will
create an environment that is equally responsive, hospitable, and
intellectually engaging for all students and faculty." Towards the end
of this section there was the complaint that ethnicity was a "cosmetic
and covert" way of avoiding ways of dealing with racism (8–9). In
addition, said McEwen, "faculty are pre-disposed against students
whose first language is not a European language."

5 This item was a complaint about a lack of formal provisions for
mentoring graduate students.

6 An assertion that the department offered a hostile and alienating
climate where students felt marginalized.

7 A complaint that there was no response to or investigation of
resignations. McEwen phrased this as follows: "Notwithstanding the
escalation, over the past three years, of withdrawals from the graduate program, including withdrawals by many of the female students, the department has failed to investigate the reason(s) why this
is happening."

8 A "lack of response to student concerns." McEwen dealt with this
in the form of an unattributed quotation: "Despite patiently making
use of all available channels (over the past three years), we have yet
to receive an effective response from the department."

9 This item read: "Atmosphere of the Department – The relationship
between faculty and students is 'authoritative,' and students are not
made to feel as though they are 'partners' in the learning experience."

WHITE MALE CULTURE

McEwen opened this discussion by commenting on the external
reviewers, who "did not deal explicitly with the students' allegations
in respect of racism and sexism, [but] their comments about the
department's culture in general are consistent with the system-wide
experiences related by the students" (21). She then cited examples of
the department's "white male culture": a lack of pluralism in the
curriculum, "dismissive and exclusionary attitudes towards feminist
and other critical approaches," one-on-one supervisory practices, and

the reference to "aggressive" mentoring (21). The strongest evidence was:

The culture of the department, as described by the external reviewers and during the interviews which I conducted, is the product of a cohort of faculty who, for the most part, are older, white, male, heterosexual, middle class, of Anglo/European cultural heritage, proud (the students would say to the point of being arrogant) of their reputation as excellent scholars, conservative in their ideological and methodological approaches, narrow rather than widely focused in their research interests, not committed to a multi-disciplinary approach, working with paradigms which are "somewhat dated," not apparently committed to fostering a more illustrious graduate program, and intensely committed to preserving their perceived long-standing "collegiality" (many of them have worked together for over twenty years); and who have been educated in the patriarchal and authoritarian traditions of Western society. (21–2)

By contrast, the graduate student culture was

the product of a more diverse group of people and interests. The student cohort includes students who are old and young, male and female, white and of colour, Canadian and international, gay, lesbian and heterosexual, interested both in mainstream and non-mainstream and critical approaches, intent upon increasing the number of female faculty and female graduate students, and intent upon opening up the curriculum to the new approaches. As well, they represent a variety of ethnic backgrounds, cultures and classes. (22)

Said McEwen by way of summary: "In the context of the Political Science Department, two such diverse cultures have been required not only to interface, but also to form a partnership in the academic community. To say that there has been a 'clash' of cultures is to state the obvious."

CURRICULUM ISSUES

The investigator did not distinguish between criticisms in the external reviews or student comments about the curriculum and the theoretical perspectives of faculty in general, and those aspects of the curriculum that pertained to the complaints of sexism and racism. In her view:

The concerned students allege that the curriculum suffers from a lack of pluralism, and that many of them have been met with hostility when their research interests and/or methods do not coincide with certain of the faculty. They assert that this has included dismissive and exclusionary attitudes towards feminist and other critical approaches. The external reviewers commented that the approaches which are dominant in the department are very much part of the mainstream and "in some ways, narrow." (21)

In addition, said Ms McEwen, the existing supervisory practice tended to emphasize a one-on-one relationship, which one reviewer had described as being excessively limiting for doctoral students. The result was that the professor might insist on the topic matching his/her expertise, and consequently "existing paradigms are likely to predominate" (21).[1]

What the students assert, in the context of allegations such as the department's intolerance towards non-mainstream perspectives, the silencing of women and people of colour in the classroom, and gender differentiation in the areas of mentoring and supervision, is that the culture and collective attitude of the department is such that it constitutes a "system," the operation of which adversely impacts on white female students as well as students of colour. That is the basis for the students' claim of pervasive sexism and racism. (23)

Further comments by the investigator included yet another reference to the word "aggressive" being linked to mentoring. The reader is reminded that an external reviewer had observed, "The use of that language in that context is an indication of a culture that may well be a 'chilly climate' for women" (17).

The University's Response

The failure of the department, the department head, the dean of arts, and the university in general to respond in ways or degrees which students deemed appropriate became an input for Ms McEwen's conclusion. She cited varous parts of the department head's letters to the dean of FOGS by way of demonstrating that the head had discredited the students and their concerns. A section on this subject, which needs several readings, was contained in the central part of the McEwen Report. I quote:

Notwithstanding the discrediting of the concerned students, as well as the minimizing of their complaints, which took place in the years and months preceding the Enquiry, the department has in fact taken certain steps –

over and above those alluded to in the Head's memoranda – which by
their nature serve to validate many of those concerns.

For example, the incoming Graduate Advisor informed me ... that
various "signs of progress" in the department should be acknowledged in
my Report ... (68)

The text continues with information from the graduate adviser's letter
and a later letter from the department head, both reporting on changes
in the curriculum and various procedures for graduate students, the
establishment of seminars on gender and policies, the reorganization
of comprehensive examination committees so that students would not
be examined by individuals against whom they had lodged human
rights complaints, and other matters. The section ended with this
summary by McEwen: "While all of these positive steps are certainly
to be acknowledged, it is nevertheless also significant to note that there
is no indication that they have been taken in the context of acknowledging the students' concerns" (69).

Additional Incidents

There were several incidents beyond the numerous specific allegations
which, together with the cultural differences in the department, provided the rationale in support of Ms McEwen's conclusions.

One of these concerned misogynist threats, which were printed in
posters hung in the Honours Reading Room (no one has alleged that
faculty were responsible). Ms McEwen said the students who reported
this were of the opinion that the university was ineffective in conducting its investigations (10).

Another allegation was that "a female MA student of colour [the
Jones case, which I described in chapter 3] filed a formal racial/sexual
harassment complaint against a faculty member. While the Head purported to take a 'hands-off approach' to the investigation of that
complaint, as well as the student's subsequent 'systemic' complaint
against the department and three additional faculty members, his
conduct was such that the student accused him of siding with the
faculty members and, hence, not providing her with a fair opportunity
to be heard" (10).

Then there was the head's responses to charges, listed under the
heading "Discrediting of the Students and their Concerns." These
responses included one to the dean of FOGS, on 6 July 1994, about
students who were not interested in a peaceful resolution and who
provided false and misleading information, and the head's memo of
19 July 1994 to faculty and students announcing the inquiry, in which

he said that public allegations of sexism and racism against three faculty members were unfounded and that the general allegations of pervasive racism and sexism were "detrimental to students, faculty, and the University" (11).

Another item concerned the opinion of the dean of FOGS (cited with much approval), including his letter of 9 June 1995 in which he informed Ms McEwen that in his opinion and to the best of his knowledge the students had acted in good faith in bringing forth comments and complaints regarding the graduate program in political science; that they had acted through appropriate channels within the university in bringing forward their complaints and in cooperating with subsequent investigations of these complaints; and that they had cooperated with the directions and/or guidelines provided to them both before and during the present inquiry (19).

Finally, there were various and selected comments of faculty members. One or another of them at some point had observed that some professors were supportive of students, that some were uncomfortable with bright, aggressive women, and that some were old-fashioned and conservative. Introspective faculty worried about being complacent, about too much in-breeding and not enough tolerance for new approaches. All such self-criticisms were taken at face value by McEwen as proof that there was a problem in this department.

SPECIFIC ALLEGATIONS

While the Report described several cases more than once in various chapters, the major allegations were restated in chapter 4 of the report. I record these below in a more succinct form, though in order to maintain a fair semblance of the way these complaints were reported by McEwen, I have retained some of the repetitious rendering and disaggregation of parts of the same complaint. There were numerous problems embedded in the Report's text to which readers should be alerted or which are worthy of note, but to avoid interrupting the narrative, I have noted only a few, inserting them as editorial notes.

However, it should be borne in mind that evidence was missing in the Report. McEwen recorded the claims but did not undertake an investigation of them. Whether the complaints were accurate or not was thus a central issue. Ms McEwen took the position that it did not matter whether they were true. What mattered was that a student apparently believed them to be true. She declared her reliance on perception.

As well, the reader should remember that the actual number of complainants whose allegations were reported by McEwen was not revealed. Many of the allegations were similar or identical to those made before the investigation (as discussed in previous chapters) by one or very few individuals. Because the complainants were anonymous, a reader unfamiliar with the department and its history would have no way of knowing whether these allegations were made by many or few students, and which allegations, now spread over many pages, were actually part of the same complaint made by a single student. Similarly, readers have no way of knowing whether the "white male professor" whose misdeeds were copiously recorded was one or many persons. The implication was that he was legion, but if the same complainant was describing the behaviour of a single professor and her complaint was spread over various categories by McEwen, the reader might reasonably assume that many "white" male professors were similarly inclined.

A. Teaching: Classroom Environment Issues and Evaluation of Students (81–5)

The first set of allegations involved "white male professors" who were said to have:

- attacked the concept of "chilly climate" and feminist theory, denounced female students who championed such views, refused to use gender-inclusive language;[2]
- failed to reprimand a rude white female for comments hurtful to a female student of colour; silenced a female undergraduate student of colour when she challenged another student on a matter pertaining to race;
- silenced white female students and/or students of colour in classroom discussions;
- were dismissive, rude, and condescending towards female undergraduate students who challenged their views;
- made rude and apparently racist comments;
- demonstrated impatience with students who "have difficulty with English";
- failed to articulate the criteria for evaluating classroom participation, "thus disadvantaging those students who typically do not enjoy the same access to it, namely the women and students of colour";[3]
- "sometimes promised as much as 30% of the final mark for classroom participation, yet treated grades achieved on written papers as being determinative of the final grade";[4]
- ignored students' requests for reforms in marking procedures; (As described in the Report, two students raised these concerns in

March 1991, but the professors "turned their backs on them and
would not participate in a constructive dialogue about the problem";
yet the minutes of a department meeting *held in March 1991*, as
reported by McEwen, recorded: "It was agreed that students should
be clearly informed at the outset of a course just how much participation will contribute to the final grade and what criteria for
assessing participation will be used. It was also agreed that students
should be given feedback about the quality of their participation
during the term" [85].)[5]
- failed to institute reforms before requested to do so by students;
  (This was the concluding allegation in the previous complaint.)
- engaged in discriminatory nonverbal behaviour such as failure to
  make eye contact with women and non-Caucasian students;
- made personal comments to students while discussing grades;
  (The comments included one to a "black"[6] female student, who was
  also the mother of small children, about the potential effect on her
  work of bearing/rearing children, and about the difficulty experienced by "women minorities" in the seminar.)
- exhibited facial language during a discussion about a student deemed
  to be "marginal," at a faculty meeting held to evaluate students;[7]
- stereotyped a student by giving her a low ranking for awards;
  (The stereotyping was alleged by a female student of colour to have
  marginalized her, and she was not assigned a department adviser.)[8]
- recommended improvements in writing English by referring students
  to the work of other students where the referred were non-Caucasian
  females and the other students were Caucasian males;
  (This is stated by McEwen as follows: "A number of instances were
  cited, in the context of grading papers, wherein professors suggested
  to female students of colour that their writing style, coherency, etc.
  was not very good, and that they should read the paper of particular
  white male students – even when the subject matter was completely
  different – in order to learn what was expected of them regarding
  the paper.")
- discriminated against a female in grading papers in one seminar.[9]

Ms McEwen concluded this part of the section on teaching with the
assertion that "in each case, there is evidence to suggest that the
student's sex and/or race may have influenced, for example, a professor's decision as to whether he would take a second look at a low
grade, the nature of the feedback given in respect of academic difficulties, and the determination of the grades to be assigned to classroom
participation. To that extent, these example [*sic*] are supportive of the
allegations of pervasive racism and sexism" (84).

B. Individual Faculty/Student Interactions (85–7)

Under this heading, McEwen stated: "As in the case of the classroom environment, the data before me supports the allegations of pervasive racism and sexism in respect of these kinds of interactions." She said that the interactions included:

- discriminatory nonverbal behaviour such as not making eye contact with white women and women of colour;
- "a white male professor chiding, in front of the other seminar students, a Jewish female PhD student who had missed her third class because of 'morning sickness' by saying that, if she missed another class, she would be expelled from the course";
- "a white male professor not acceding to the request of a female Jewish PhD student to defer presenting her paper because her presentation date fell on an important religious holiday" (when, for religious reasons, she was unable to use any means of transportation);
- an insensitive response to an undergraduate female student who requested an extension for a paper because of her grandmother's funeral;
- an insensitive and rude comment to an undergraduate female student who explained her absence from class;
- an insensitive and rude comment to an undergraduate female who came to see a professor about a grade assigned by the teaching assistant;
- an insensitive comment to an undergraduate female student who was considering application to the MA program;
- "a hostile and authoritarian response" to a female student of colour who, wishing to audit a seminar, arrived late.

Ms McEwen concluded this section: "These examples lend support, in my opinion, to the allegations of pervasive racism and sexism in the area of individual faculty/student interactions."

C. The Intellectual Climate and Curriculum (87–9)

The complaint here was that faculty tended to be intolerant of "non-mainstream, critical, and non-disciplinary approaches" to their subject. Examples given:

- the introduction of alternative perspectives in a "decontextualized way";

- "a female professor of colour failing to include, in her undergraduate class called 'Women and Development,' materials written by 'third world feminist writers.' A female undergraduate student of colour described the course as 'tokenism' and said that most of it was taken up by 'Western feminism.' She described the course as 'just a perpetuation of stereotypes,' and 'not enlightening'";
- failure to include sufficient Third World writers in undergraduate reading lists, and teaching the courses from the perspective of white Western scholars;
- Eurocentric attitudes towards Aboriginal peoples;
- the stereotyping of Islamic religion by both a white male professor and a white female professor in two separate undergraduate Third World courses;
- refusal to mark a paper "written by a lesbian undergraduate student of colour which challenged heterosexual assumptions";
- a statement made to a Jewish female professor by a white male professor that feminism is a "Jewish-American Princess conspiracy";
- failure to broaden course curricula beyond a "narrow, ethnocentric 'very male, and very white' base" in the subfield of political theory;
- agreement between a white male professor and a white male MA student during classroom discussion when the student called feminism a point of view and not a theoretical approach;
- failure to encourage students to take courses in other departments or otherwise to expand contacts with scholars elsewhere in the university;
- discouragement of critical thinking; encouragement of submissive behaviour.

D. *Inappropriate Socializing and Sexual/Racial Harassment (89–94)*

The following examples were cited by female students about "white male professors" who were said to have:

- informed an applicant to the department that he would facilitate her application if she went out with him;
- made a sexual advance after having lunch and drinks with the student;
- invited female students out on dates, tried to discuss their romantic life with them, and generally "came on" to them;
- winked "while suggesting to a mature white female PhD student that, if a seminar at his home runs late, 'you can always stay over'";
- made a sexual advance to a female undergraduate student of colour who was working as a research assistant;

- asked a "female PhD student of colour, during the oral part of her comprehensive examination, to distinguish between 'discourse' and 'intercourse'";
- posted sexist and crude cartoons on his office door;
- in a classroom, compared "nuclear radiation and a woman's sexual appetite";
- joked to a "female colleague about a professor he had when he was a student who preferred the theatre-style classrooms because he could look up the skirts of his female students";
- joked "with undergraduate students 'over a beer' about a suggestion made by a white male professor to him to the effect that he should 'get a female student as a collaborator on your book. Then, you could be working on the book while she could be working on something else'";
- gazed "persistently" at the chest area of female students;
- interrupted conversations with students to look at female students;
- interrupted "a conversation between a female PhD student of colour and a female member of the support staff by walking between the two of them, 'hip-checking' the support person against the wall, saying 'hey baby!' to her and then proceeding down the hall";
- made personal comments about hairstyle or other features of female appearance;
- discriminated in the treatment of students for tardy arrival at class or for late papers (excusing males, chastising or penalizing females);
- discriminated with respect to socializing (e.g., a male student was invited to meet a distinguished journalist while a female was not).

White male faculty were the major focus of attention for this category of complaints, but fellow students were also faulted, especially with reference to various antifeminist taunting and verbal and visual sexual harassment of female honours students by males.

E. Mentoring and Thesis Supervision (94–9)

General complaints were expressed about differential treatment whereby male students received more encouragement, information, and opportunities to advance. One example of differential attitudes was as follows: "When a white female PhD student was awarded one of the Killam scholarships in 1990 (given only to the top University Graduate Fellowship applicants), no formal announcement was made to members of the department regarding her achievement. Notwithstanding that fact, the Head, just a few weeks later, circulated a memorandum congratulating the (white male) University Graduate Fellowship recipients."

Other examples of differential treatment, again all referring to "white male professors," were that the professor had:

- "'told a white Jewish female MA student' who worried about the lack of career opportunities, that she 'could try being a waitress or being a go-go dancer'";
- reacted "dismissively when a white female PhD student asked him to read a paper that he knew had been accepted for" a conference and had received a high grade from another professor;
- rebuked a white female PhD student for her absence from an informal meeting when he knew that she was absent in order to present a paper elsewhere;
- omitted the name of a white female PhD student on a conference program where she was a paper presenter.

Several examples refer to faculty-student colloquia. Ms McEwen summarized these: "In one case, a black female PhD student was singled out as a representative of her particular ethnic group, in another a female MA student of colour was sexualized, and – the last example – a white female PhD student was interrupted and her contribution to the discussion demeaned." More detailed information on these cases was then given:

- "In the first case, a black female PhD student stated that, at a colloquium held in November of 1990, the speaker, a white male professor in the department, gave a racist response to a question that she asked. The professor had suggested, in his presentation, that technology represented a liberating instrument in international relations. When the student asked how that view could be reconciled with the 'two-way, free flow of communication debate' (a debate which involves the question of whether technology is in fact just another form of imperialism), the professor responded by way of a *non-sequitur*, stating that Africans will not always be 'down,' and that black people in Africa are dying of AID's [*sic*]. When the student restated her question, commenting that she must not have articulated the question very well, the professor responded by saying words to the effect of 'You must not feel so badly about the black and oppressed. They will not always be down.'"
- "A white male professor stood with his arm around a female MA student of colour while talking at a colloquium to a group of students and faculty members, and, later, while introducing her to the guest speaker."
- "At another colloquium, a white male professor 'spoke over' the comments made to the guest speaker by a white female PhD student,

following which the speaker was dismissive of the student's comments. When the student later complained to the professor about his behaviour, he responded by saying 'that's just the way that academic dialogue goes.'"

There were various complaints about advice and process relating to thesis supervision, including one about a "white female PhD student, a past winner of a Killam scholarship and ranked 'excellent' by the department, being met with hostility on the part of a white female professor when she elected to change her area of study. After having produced a number of thesis proposals, only to have each one of them rejected by her (white male professor) supervisor, the student decided to change her area of study as well as her supervisor."

The female professor was said to have responded "angrily" when the student phoned her about this, and to have informed the graduate adviser in writing that she was displeased with the student's behaviour. She said that the student's telephone conversation "was alternatively self-pitying, sarcastic, bullying, and rude" and that the student "persists in viewing my position not in terms of academic standards and credibility, but in personal terms such as not 'liking her,' not 'caring,' thinking she is 'stupid,' not being 'fair,' etc. I am sorry it has come to this, but as a result, I would find it difficult to work with her." The student characterized the female professor's response as sexist.

F. The Graduate Program (99–103)

In every university department, comprehensive examinations are the source of great anxiety and sometimes the cause of grief and withdrawal from graduate programs. The complaints in political science included two from women who had withdrawn. The first was described as a "Jewish female PhD" who was required to write her comprehensive too soon after the birth of her baby, who failed it and also failed the rewrite six months later, and attributed her failure to being refused a deferral by a white male professor. The second case involved a "female PhD student of colour" who felt that she had been given insufficient information before an examination, who failed it, failed the rewrite, and was forced to withdraw. A detailed list of complaints from the second student included the information that a white male professor had spent time coaching a "male student of colour" who also had failed the first examination, but that he had refused to spend time helping her. As well, the examination was deferred from the end of November to January, an arrangement that was not to her benefit because she had domestic and teaching assistantship duties through December and could not study; she believed the extended time enabled the male student to pass.

There were also complaints about teaching assistantship roles. A "white female PhD student" alleged that she was criticized unfairly for her nonconformist marking standards as a teaching assistant; a "white female MA student" alleged that her supervisor had said to her, "You are likely a soft marker," which she took to be a sexist comment. A "female MA student of colour" alleged that her "white male supervisor" supervised her more than the "two white male" teaching assistants for the course. A professor phoned a student "late one Sunday evening" but terminated the call when another telephone in his home was picked up.

Another dispute was that of Jones, reported earlier. McEwen's description of the infamous remark runs this way:

The professor responded to the female Teaching Assistant's comment to the effect that the undergraduate students whose papers she had just marked for the first time would likely now start to respect her, by saying: "Yeah, now they know that you are one big, bad, black, bitch." In the face of the student's shocked and silent reaction to that remark, her supervisor nevertheless proceeded to press her – over the next several days – to attend a "beer session" which he was sponsoring for the winners of the simulation exercise. (102)

Information in the graduate student survey indicates a differential by gender in the allocation of funding. In addition, part-time students ("most typically female") have low access to funding. McEwen notes a curious disjuncture between two major sources of funding: the university graduate fellowships and the Social Science and Humanities Research Council of Canada fellowships. No gender differences showed up on the first, but the success rate for males on the second was said to be "substantially higher" than for females (no data were provided). McEwen attributed this to unfair grading of students for ranked lists that go to SSHRCC, but since the two allocations normally depend on the same ranked lists, that cannot explain the alleged difference. Further, statistics provided by the department showed no gender differentiation in grading, and McEwen noted this.

G. High Attrition Rate of PhD Women (103–5)

According to the allegations submitted in 1992 and 1993, there had been a "dramatic decline" in the number of female PhD students and an escalation in the withdrawal rate. McEwen correctly reported that ten out of twenty-six female students (including three of colour) had left the graduate program between 1977 and 1993. In the same period, eight women, including two of colour, had received their PhDs. McEwen does not report that three of the women who had left had failed examinations, as had three men; four women withdrew voluntarily, as did fifteen men; and three women left because of transfer to other universities or because of medical leave; one male left because he did not complete a thesis (see table 5 in chap. 4). McEwen said that she interviewed those who had withdrawn and "almost all" had "experienced direct and systemic forms of sexism and either experienced or observed direct and systemic forms of racism."

H. Female Faculty (105–6)

In 1992 the department had twenty-two tenure-stream faculty, of whom three were female; and in 1994 it had twenty-five tenure-stream faculty, of whom five were female. Not all males or females were full-time, since some had joint appointments. In 1994 there were twenty-one full-time faculty, of whom three were female. Thus, about one-quarter of tenure-stream and one-seventh of full-time faculty were women by 1994, compared with about one-twelfth in 1992. Another way of measuring this is to count full-time equivalents; by this measure, in 1994 there were 23.5 full-time equivalents, of whom 3.8 were female.[10]

McEwen said that the "number of female faculty remains disproportionately low," and that "while four of the hires in the last five years have been women (two of them women of colour), a trend which reflects that the department is now taking the appropriate and necessary steps to correct the current gender imbalance on the faculty, the imbalance nevertheless continues to create problems." In relation to the problems, she cited the external reports that complained of the gender imbalance as of 1992. Without offering specific examples, she said that female faculty members felt excluded and unfairly treated by their male colleagues.

I. Female Support Staff (107)

Finally there were the female support staff who, according to McEwen, "were reluctant to say anything" – which fact she attributed to fear of reprisals. She said that "while expressions of strong support for the department and all of the faculty were made by some [staff members], others expressed concerns and provided examples about the sexist way in which they are treated by certain of the faculty" (107).

MCEWEN'S CONCLUSIONS (107–13)

The case against the male "white" faculty was now complete, and Ms McEwen turned to the failure of the department head and the dean of arts to do something about it. She observed that when the students complained in June 1992, "they were met with a non-supportive, authoritative [sic] and, in fact, obstructionist environment. Not only were those very serious allegations never investigated; they were not even acknowledged" (107).

The head was charged with failure to act, denial of wrongdoing, defence of his faculty members, and failure to acknowledge problems. "With respect to the allegations of systemic discrimination, faculty either denied that any discrimination had occurred, cited statistical information aimed at refuting the claims being made, and/or pointed to the 'success' of white females and students of colour as proof that racism and sexism do not pervade the department. By failing to acknowledge the systemic and pervasive nature of the concerns, the administration and the faculty required students to dismantle those holistic concepts, allege watertight incidents, and prove the 'guilt' of individual respondents" (108).

With reference to the statistical and other data provided as refutation of the students' claims, McEwen agreed that the departmental statistics showed no gender disparity in drop-out rates of male and female MA students, and that they showed a higher admission rate of female than male students into the graduate program and no gender differentiation in the area of overall grading (110). But she argued that other responses from the department were not valid. For example, there remained the high attrition rate of female PhD students, in both absolute and relative terms.

McEwen argued that even though the student evaluations administered in March 1994 gave positive responses, the department was not good at ensuring that students took them seriously, and anyway there was a "leniency bias" built into this form of evaluation. "People are wary of publically [sic] criticizing those whom they know personally" was her explanation of the results of evaluations by more than 1,400 students in all classes.

McEwen's position on statistical evidence generally was that it "compartmentalized into watertight compartments" the profound concerns of systemic and other forms of discrimination, and that it was used to dismantle those concerns "scientifically" (111). With statistical evidence treated as irrelevant in this way, Ms McEwen said: "In no way to detract from those ways in which the department is demonstrating

fair and equitable treatment of its students, I would note that – just
because an organization is acting in a non-discriminatory manner in
some respects – does not mean that it is acting in a non-discriminatory
manner in every respect" (111). This judgment echoes comments made
earlier in the Report where McEwen condemned the department both
for failing to respond to complaints and for changing procedures in
response to them (68–9).

THE PRESIDENT'S INSTANT DECISION

As dean of arts, I received a copy of the Report on Sunday, 18 June
1995. Early the following morning, at a meeting of the group of
administrators who had deliberated over the terms of reference a year
earlier, I was informed that the president, acting on the recommendations of the dean of FOGS, had already accepted all the Report's
recommendations, including the suspension of admissions to graduate
studies, and that his decision was non-negotiable. However, I and
others were permitted to make some slight modifications to the word-
ing of his proposed press release. The president announced his decision
publicly in a press conference on 19 June 1995 and through a letter
to the entire campus community dated 21 June. McEwen's seven major
recommendations were restated by the president in his announcement
that he would take the following measures:

1 suspension of admissions to the graduate program in the Department
  of Political Science, to remain in effect until "there are satisfactory
  provisions in place relating to educational equity and a learning and
  working environment which is free from harassment and discrimination";
2 dissemination of the Report to each graduate student in the Department and to those already admitted for the following year;
3 prohibition of retaliation against students, staff, or faculty as a result
  of their participation in the inquiry; "Further, where evidence exists
  which suggests that retaliatory action has occurred or may occur,
  the University will investigate the matter and, if the charge is sub-
  stantiated, appropriate disciplinary or corrective action will be
  taken";
4 the vice-president, Academic, and the provost to strike a committee
  to define clearly the respective roles and responsibilities of various
  administrators regarding jurisdictions pertaining to graduate students;
5 the new policy on discrimination and harassment to be the principal
  vehicle for combatting discrimination and harassment;

6 the university to negotiate with the faculty association regarding a joint statement on creation of an environment free from harassment and discrimination;

7 the Equity Office (which had come into existence in 1994) to serve an ombudslike function.

If the administrators supposed that their quick capitulation would dull the response, they were far off the mark. The ensuing debate was acrimonious on all sides, and everyone came out of it looking the worse for wear. The university suffered enormous loss of prestige and credibility. The faculty became angry and demoralized, whichever position they took on specific issues. Even donors expressed their dismay with the president's decision (and their dismay hurt most of all).

CHAPTER SEVEN

Reactions

In accordance with the administration's promise to the graduate students, the Report was distributed to all enrolled and incoming graduate students and all faculty in the Department of Political Science, to all heads and directors in the faculty, to all deans, and to virtually anyone else who requested a copy. Several hundred copies were distributed to the media, other universities, and individuals on request. Reactions were swift in coming and came from all directions.

IMMEDIATE REACTIONS

Readers of newspapers but not of the Report must have become confused by the divergent versions of what the Report contained. Journalists selected examples according to the slant of their story, their personal bias, or the bias of their newspaper. Karen Gram of the *Vancouver Sun*, in an article sympathetic to the graduate students, included a two-column box highlighting "some of the incidents of sexism and racism cited" in the Report.[1] These alleged incidents included forms of sexism such as male professors asking female students for dates, putting their arms around them, or talking about their clothes and appearance.[2] Meanwhile, Nicole Parten, also at the *Vancouver Sun*, had a different "take" on the Report and focused on Jones's non-negotiable demands in an article that appeared two days after the Gram piece. Parten also quoted the president of the political science (undergraduate) students' association – a Sikh woman – who said that she disagreed with McEwen's conclusions and thought the department head was "most considerate" and "very approachable."[3]

Some graduate students cheered when the Report backed their claims. The graduate student who had failed her comprehensives in political science and then transferred successfully to another department (and who had been contacted by the dean of FoGS prior to the writing of the second letter in 1993) was quoted in the Gram piece as saying, "Students are expecting the university to go beyond the recommendations and institute schedules for remedies." Gram reported that this student claimed to have been "harassed out" of the department and that she envisioned remedies that would include "tuition rebates, re-evaluation of grades or the allocation of funds that have been improperly denied them"; as reported by Gram, she said that the department had been in a state of civil war since the beginning of the McEwen investigation.

The ecstacy of some of the graduate students was matched in intensity by the harshness of some of the critics, the *Globe and Mail* leading the way. Extracts were published there in a lengthy editorial headed "UBC's Brush with Political Correctness," which said in part:

Doubt that there is an epidemic of political correctness at Canadian universities? Think that all the talk of McCarthyism is a touch overdone? Transport yourself for a moment to the campus of the University of British Columbia, where a report has just been completed on alleged sexism and racism in the department of political science. It is a bone-chilling document – made even more so by the university's craven response ...

In all the numbing reams of this report, there is not one solid proof that any UBC professor treated one student as inferior to another on the basis of race or sex, much less that those students suffered genuine disadvantage as a consequence ...

Laced with Orwellian euphemisms, reeking of the worst forms of political correctness, lacking the slightest respect for due process, Ms. McEwen's report is a cowardly, disgraceful thing. A strong university president would have said as much.[4]

Meanwhile, the Society for Academic Freedom and Scholarship wrote an open letter to the president, expressing its "utmost concern" and saying that it viewed his action as "a gross and unwarranted assault on the academic freedom of your faculty, and furthermore, of students – both those in your university and those who are considering entering it. It suggests to all observers that under your leadership, the University of British Columbia is prepared to sacrifice due process and basic principles of fairness at the altar of political correctness." Similarly, the president of the UBC Faculty Association condemned the Report, saying that it lacked evidence and that the complaints cited had less to do with sexual and racial discrimination than with the normal tensions of graduate life. Later, the executive of the association resolved "to request the President to rescind the present penalty."

The Alliance of Feminists across Campuses, however, issued an anonymous denunciation against the faculty members, who it believed had given the name and address of Ms Jones to an inquiring reporter (the faculty flatly denied having done so).[5] The alliance used the occasion of its broadsheet to claim that there was a backlash "orchestrated, we have no doubt, by the very faculty and administrators who are critiqued in the report." Curiously, the UBC president and the Faculty Association president were named as culprits along with faculty in political science.

JULY: THE DEBATE CONTINUES

The debate became more heated along with the summer sun. Twenty-two faculty members wrote to the *Vancouver Sun* on 5 July 1995 to disclaim any support for the critical statements made by the president of the Faculty Association. They spoke of the need for an "inclusive and non-discriminatory climate" and congratulated the political science students who had had "the courage to come forward with their experiences of racism and sexism."

I myself contributed to the heat by writing a letter to the university newspaper, largely in response to the letter from the twenty-two faculty members, though I did not refer to it. My letter said in part:

As the Dean of the Faculty involved in this unfortunate affair, and also as a female member of faculty, I am entirely in agreement with the sentiment that we should strive to create an inclusive and non-discriminatory climate at UBC. There are problems to be addressed in the Political Science and in other departments. Toward the goal of improving the "climate" for all students, faculty, and staff, the Faculty of Arts is developing guidelines for heads, deans, and faculty, and is undertaking debate on these sensitive issues. The department of Political Science has dedicated itself to becoming a more sensitive community.

To recognize the need to institute reforms and become more sensitive to the issues does not preclude and is not in conflict with another recognition, namely that the Report is deeply flawed. Among many weaknesses: it dismisses testimony and evidence contrary to the allegations and relegates faculty responses to a short appendix; evidence is lacking; allegations are repeated as if all were about sexism and racism even where there is no apparent or necessary linkage, and the context of alleged comments is not reported. The investigator failed to distinguish between the taking of offense and provable harm related to complaints, and did not define "systemic" discrimination in terms of harmful practice. There is a persistent assumption of guilt by virtue of accusation. The Report, in short, is deficient in principles of natural justice, a deficiency that does not in the long run serve the interests of the aggrieved any more than of the defendants.

Lead editorials in both the *Globe and Mail* (strongly supportive) and the *Vancouver Sun* (lukewarm to hostile) considered my arguments, and some newspapers reprinted my letter in full or in part. On a spate of radio shows I said that I favoured conscious efforts to improve the climate for women and for minority groups on campus, but that I found this Report repugnant because of its bias, lack of evidence, and basic injustice. In this I felt fairly certain that I had the support of most faculty members in arts.

Other faculties dealt with the conflict by keeping it at a distance. Only two deans spoke up during the long summer. The dean of education wrote a strongly supportive (public) letter to the president. She called his decision "prompt and courageous" and the McEwen Report a "wake-up" pill. The dean of commerce wrote a strongly critical letter to the president, calling for removal of the embargo on graduate admissions to political science. He made it clear that his objection was to the flawed Report and the inappropriate response, and not to the principle of equity. The vice-president, Academic, wrote a letter to the *Globe and Mail*, but he made no memorable argument in it.[6] The vice-president, Student Services, spoke up in several forums on behalf of students. No other deans or vice-presidents spoke in public.

They kept silence for several reasons. Most did so because it was dangerous to speak out; one was easily labelled immoral, sexist, and racist if one disapproved publicly of the Report. In faculties where there were both outspoken defenders of McEwen and outspoken defenders of academic freedom, it was safer to keep silent than get caught in the crossfire. For some academics in the applied sciences, the political and philosophical context of the debate was such unknown territory that they simply had no capacity to judge the issues. Besides, most people, including administrators, were totally puzzled by the whole affair. As noted earlier, no one approved of sexism and racism, no one wanted to support such behaviour or excuse it, and few were willing to trust their own judgment about the Report to say one way or the other whether the department was guilty as charged. Finally, there were some who simply backed a president on principle, irrespective of the issues.

My intervention had some positive effect on the subsequent debate in the Faculty of Arts, however, because now it was possible for both women and men who strongly opposed discrimination to admit openly that this Report and the university's response were not reasonable ways to eliminate offences. I was deluged with letters over the rest of the summer, the vast majority of them positive and supportive.

Twenty-four department heads and program chairs in the Faculty of Arts sent a letter to the Board of Governors and the president calling for removal of the suspension. They spoke of the "widespread dissatisfaction with the Report arising from its general disregard of principles of natural justice as they affect both the Faculty and Graduate Students" and the unbalanced nature of the Report. They concluded: "The Faculty strongly believes that the University was mistaken in acting upon the basis of a fundamentally flawed report with insufficient consultation with the Dean of Arts, the Head and the faculty of Political Science about the allegations contained in the report, and in taking precipitous and drastic action, which has compromised the university's commitment to due process."

These faculty leaders consciously stated their continued support for measures to eliminate discrimination and create a more supportive environment for all members of the university community; indeed, in this and several other communications they openly admitted to problems in current practices. Their opposition to the Report and to the suspension of graduate admissions in political science was not rooted in antifeminism or hostility towards reform, but in their anger at the lack of due process.

The president was unmoved by this petition. Petitions were also sent from the entire resident faculty in psychology and the entire resident faculty in economics. Petitions from groups of individuals were sent to the president and the Board of Governors, but none altered the path the president had chosen. Although the board indicated its intention to invite both the deans to its next meeting, only the dean of FoGS actually received an invitation; thus I, as dean of arts, was not able to present the argument of the department heads in person.[7]

Although it was midsummer, a time when many faculty members were away on holiday or on research ventures, more than one hundred turned up on 13 July for an informal meeting of the Faculty of Arts to discuss the Report. This meeting was strongly supportive of the stance that I and their department heads had taken.

In the same week that my letter was published, the B.C. Civil Liberties Association delivered its judgment on the Report: "Badly flawed, and the University's response to it unwarranted and unfairly damaging to the Department, to the faculty members of the Department, and (perhaps most importantly) to the free expression of ideas in the university community."[8] The association noted, among its many critical comments, that in the thirty-two pages of repetitive allegations, the preponderance were "minor in nature" and did "not obviously provide a basis for a claim of racism or sexism"; further, that although the Report spoke frequently of "racist and sexist" behaviour, most of the allegations were about sexism: "Even by Ms. McEwen's weak test, it is questionable whether there is any support at all for the allegation of racism in the Department."

The association argued that there was a serious logical flaw in McEwen's reasoning. It posed the hypothetical problem: suppose that graduate students were accepted into the program who wanted to learn feminist perspectives; suppose that the white, male, late-middle-aged faculty were deficient as teachers of feminism; suppose that all the students who wanted to study feminism were women and/or members of minority groups. If all these suppositions were true, would it follow that faculty were racist and sexist? The association answered negatively. It might possibly follow that the department should not have accepted into its program persons whose interests could not be met by faculty, or that faculty were not renewing themselves and keeping up to date. But there is quite a difference between being racist and sexist and having inadequate controls on student intake or being pedagogically out of date. Finally, the association argued that the president's response was "patently unfair," unprecedented, and irresponsible. In its view, the students were short-changed, because no genuine investigation had taken place and the individual complaints had not been dealt with; the reputation of faculty members had been unfairly tarnished; and the wider world of academics had had its freedom to learn and teach severely threatened.

There were contrary voices that were equally impassioned. In midsummer these were not the dominant themes in the morality play, but they became louder as time went on. Spokespersons for the Graduate Student Society were particularly strident in denouncing faculty who dismissed the Report on the grounds that it infringed their own academic freedom. The society argued that students had less freedom than faculty, and claimed that faculty had criticized the form of the Report in order to deflect attention from the substantive issues.[9] These spokespersons allowed for no possibility that those who dismissed the Report were neither defending their academic bailiwicks nor trying to deflect attention from the issues. In this respect, they took a position similar to that of the president; he, too, refused to acknowledge other grounds for opposition.

Two student newspapers – the Graduate Student Society's newsletter and the *Ubyssey* – mounted massive attacks of an *ad feminam* variety. In their view, I had criticized the Report solely to deflect attention from the real problems of sexism and racism. These papers continued throughout the entire episode to tear into me and the Faculty of Arts, which was characterized as sexist, racist, conservative, and unwilling to work cooperatively with students. On the couple of occasions that

I answered calls from the *Ubyssey* (the graduate students' newsletter never called to check any of its versions), I perceived (a term now made acceptable to students by McEwen) that the reporters were rude to me, so I stopped responding to phone calls.

A spokeswoman for the major support-staff union on campus expressed and disseminated a view which no doubt many others held. She thought that the two deans had written the terms of reference all by themselves, had chosen to keep everything anonymous, and had refused to consult with graduate students – and that now the dean of arts was complaining because the Report did not say what she wanted. This is how it must have appeared to many people, but there was little point in trying to describe the actual process or what it was the dean of arts was complaining about when no other administrators present at the various meetings would speak up.

Stephen Hume, a leading *Vancouver Sun* columnist, wrote a thoughtful piece about sexism in our society, in which he agreed that my objections to the Report were "reasonable ... if the report were intended to be the basis for disciplinary action." But he felt that the Report itself needed to be taken seriously as a depiction of a widespread problem at universities and other institutions.[10] He thought men's rejection of it was a "knee-jerk" response. Hume understood the nature of sexism; unfortunately, he showed no comprehension of the nature of due process.

THE PRESIDENT'S LETTER OF 4 AUGUST

In August, following a directive from the Board of Governors, the president wrote a letter to the whole campus. The board's directive was that he should distance himself from the Report and mollify the critics, but the president's letter instead intensified the opposition to his actions. He admitted that the McEwen Report was flawed, but he then stated that even so, "the University felt it had to act." He apologized to students. He avoided any reference to the debate over due process and justice, and focused – as he had from the beginning – on academic freedom for students. He said in part:

One perspective interprets these events as the sacrifice of academic freedom on the altar of political correctness. Another accuses the University administration of taking lightly its obligation to protect the academic freedom of students to express ideas or points of view without fear of racist or sexist responses. Neither point of view is correct.

At the heart of the Report is the conclusion that "both in terms of substance and of process" the evidence supports "allegations of pervasive racism and sexism" (p. 113). Much confusion, I believe, arises because there are undoubted flaws in the Report; for example, it conflates serious charges with trivial ones, and its narrative style lacks tight, reasoned, integrated analysis of all the evidence. In addition, a general report on the "climate" in the department, not assessing individual fault, can be read as implicating all faculty, some unfairly.

However, despite the limitations of the Report the University felt it had to act. Indeed, the Report's limitations serve to obscure, not eliminate, the basic reality that the Political Science department must confront its learning environment which has been found (not only in the McEwen Report) to constitute a serious impediment to learning and discourse.

This has not arisen, as the Report recognizes, because there was any intent to discriminate. Nonetheless, this situation has, I believe, created an issue of academic freedom with which the University community must be concerned. To its credit, the Department of Political Science has acknowledged that this is an issue it must and will confront.

We are therefore committed to addressing the problems that have been acknowledged to exist.

In a subsequent interview with CBC investigative reporter Joe Schlesinger, the president distanced himself from the suspension. He told Schlesinger on film that the dean of FOGS had imposed it and that only that dean could undo it.

Both the department and the dean of arts objected strenuously to the president's August letter. In a meeting (at my request) and in a subsequent letter, I pointed out that if the president had other information not so far disclosed, as his letter suggested, he was obliged to make it known and provide for a defence. If he had no other information, then his letter was misleading and he should publicly withdraw it. He eventually acknowledged my letter but did not respond to it. However, in response to a similar letter from the acting head of the department, he admitted that he had no other information; but he did not withdraw anything. The acting head pointed out that the department's civility, considering the nature of the Report and the president's actions, was now being characterized as an admission of guilt. In fact, faculty members had accepted a vow of public silence while its members met almost daily with one another and with students to come to grips with the issues.

PUBLIC OPINION SWINGS: AUGUST, SEPTEMBER

Although the president's letter caused Tom Berger to resign from the Board of Governors, its more general effect was to embolden the defenders of his decision. Timing is everything in the game of public persuasion, and the pendulum of opinion had reached its arc on the critical periphery; now it began its swing back. In line with the president's rationale, those who defended the imposition of penalties on the Department of Political Science were distancing themselves from the McEwen Report and claiming that there were other reasons for the president's actions.

People began to speak of personal feelings, personal experiences, personal beliefs – whether about life in general or the Department of Political Science in particular – and to reach unabashed conclusions on the basis of these beliefs. During the early fall I met several women who earnestly told me about racism and sexism to which they had been exposed in other places at other times; apparently, they believed that their own experiences justified the penalties in this case. These women were prominent – on the Board of Governors, in the faculty, in the media – and their experiential version of events moved others to condemn the department even if they had not read the Report. Men spoke of other men's rapacious activities; they distanced themselves by casting stones at the political scientists.

In addition, a story was circulating far and wide to the effect that McEwen had failed to uncover the truth and that the truth was far worse than anything she had written. I heard from colleagues in Toronto and Edmonton about the presence of "two or three" men in the department whose exploits were said to be particularly obscene. The speakers had no idea who these men might be, but they had heard rumours across the mountains. I am willing to believe that there are some people in most medium-sized university departments (or in the departments of any other organization) whose behaviour is less than ideal; but since McEwen tried every imaginable route to uncover these anonymous individuals in the Department of Political Science and apparently failed, I find it hard to believe that their real exploits lived up to the well-publicized fantasies.

There were also stories about faculty men who had married students, and certainly there were at least two such cases in the department; there were four in another department, and going around the faculty I could identify others, including several prominent scholars and administrators whose spouses were former students. There is good reason to curb relations between faculty and students as long as the faculty members have power over the students and the students' cohort (since it is unfair to the cohort if one member of the class has a privileged position). But an institution can go only so far to curb romance; universities are places that typically employ young faculty to teach young students, and romances are fairly normal human outcomes.

These men were no longer youngsters, however, and I wondered if any of the stories was of recent vintage. One of the "shocking" revelations posed by McEwen during her interviews turned out to be about a relationship that had blossomed some two decades earlier. She dropped it from the Report, which was just as well; it seemed a bit late to indulge in punishment.

Women were particularly affected by the stories going around. Some genuinely believed that these particular men were guilty; others believed that most men were malefactors so catching a few of them was not a bad idea and served as a warning to others (maybe as a "wake-up call," to use the words of the dean of education). One university administrator publicly stated that she did not really care if these men were guilty; punishing them would be a way of getting the message across to the campus that sexism would no longer be tolerated.

Meanwhile, external groups were being encouraged to write on behalf of the warring factions. It was fair enough for the UBC Graduate Student Society to obtain the endorsement of the National Graduate Council in Ottawa, for the UBC Faculty Association had obtained the endorsement of the Canadian Association of University Teachers, the

Society for Academic Freedom and Scholarship, and the B.C. Civil
Liberties Union. I myself joined others in asking the Royal Society of
Canada to conduct a study of the process and create an advisory
document either pertaining to the events at UBC or to inquiries in
general. So I was not surprised to hear that the National Graduate
Council fully and unreservedly supported McEwen, the complainants,
and the UBC Graduate Student Society.

As noted above, there were also those who defended McEwen by
mounting *ad feminam* attacks in my direction. That I was being
"defensive" was one that puzzled me, but that I was "covering up"
something was at least understandable, even if it was untrue. Persistently my position was characterized by those who wanted no debate
on the Report as antifeminist, though nothing could have been further
from the truth. I had intimations of the anger some graduate students
and others who supported them now felt for me, of course, but I
confess my breath was taken away by a cartoon that appeared in
October, on the day of both a Faculty of Arts meeting and a meeting
of the Graduate Council, an advisory body to the dean of FoGS. It was
posted prominently throughout the Graduate Student Centre and subsequently reprinted in the *Vancouver Sun* alongside a lengthy column
by Stephen Hume against the lifting of the suspension.

GRADUATE STUDENTS, POLITICAL SCIENCE

Meanwhile, the graduate students in the department tried to find
common ground, but their personal relationships had been poisoned
by the inquiry. Their battles were royal and were widely reported
throughout the faculty. In a letter to the president dated 15 August, I
brought the matter to his attention:

Current graduate students are not homogeneous in their views about these
matters. It is not sufficient at this stage to imagine that students' interests
are well served by the Report or the President's decision. Honesty and a
sense of political reality demand that we recognize students as a highly
diverse group with differing perspectives. I remind you that in spite of all
the advertising for the McEwen Inquiry, fewer than half the students
actually chose to be interviewed by her and her definition of students who
had complaints included persons with complaints that had nothing at all
to do with the charges of sexism and racism.

My attempts to change the course fell on deaf ears, but the *Globe
and Mail* managed to attract attention when it published a draft
of proposals written by one of the graduate student complainants

(referred to in my earlier chapters as Ms Keate, and by McEwen as a "mature female student"). How the newspaper obtained it I do not know, though I am fairly confident that no faculty members sent it because few had copies at that time; and those who did were conscientiously following a general strategy of keeping a lid on the department. The last thing they wanted was further media exposure. As reported in the *Globe and Mail*, the student advocated in part:

- a formal, public, written acceptance of the McEwen Report and a formal apology by faculty, both of which were to be published;
- re-education for faculty (a twelve-step recovery program was recommended);
- early retirement for the recalcitrant;
- selection of a new department head by a committee that would include the dean of graduate studies, graduate students, and faculty who had demonstrated their support for the McEwen Report;
- the removal of incompetent instructors, including two people who were identified by name; and
- financial and mentoring aid for any students who considered withdrawing from the program.[11]

This report brought forth a predictable spate of articles in defence of academic freedom, and it encouraged the *B.C. Report* to renew its attack, now comparing the students to Red Guards.[12] It also encouraged the formation of a British Columbian branch of the Society for Academic Freedom and Scholarship. A psychology professor referred to the "reeducation" campaign as "in danger of becoming a witch hunt" and said that it reminded him of "the worst excesses of the Cultural Revolution in China."[13] Emotions were running so high that when a faculty member married a *Vancouver Sun* journalist, the couple found it necessary to issue a press release to allay the criticism from some of the students.

THE UNIVERSITY SENATE MEETING, 19 SEPTEMBER 1995

The Faculty of Arts continued to agitate against the McEwen Report and the suspension, and a motion was put forward for a special meeting early in September to consider requesting the president to lift the suspension. By this time other groups on campus, including the Graduate Student Society and the Academic Women's Association, had developed momentum in the opposite direction. Faculty members with opposing opinions attended the meeting, together with student representatives. After two hours of impassioned though remarkably civil debate, the vote was ninety-seven in favour and fifty-two opposed to a motion to request that the president remove the suspension on graduate admissions to the Department of Political Science. The result of the vote was delivered to the president, who did not respond, though he was reported to have said that this was not the business of the Faculty of Arts. The result was also sent to the dean of FoGS who later, at a senate meeting, characterized it as merely an opinion and therefore carrying no authority.

The atmosphere became increasingly tense thereafter, and it was especially so at the university senate meeting on 19 September. The senate was the appropriate body to impose discipline on a department, particularly in a case such as this, and the fact that the dean of FoGS and the president had failed to bring the matter to the senate at its first fall meeting (it does not meet during the summer) had aroused much anger. In advance of this meeting, instead of putting an open motion before the senate, the president's office compiled a group of items supporting his position: a report from the dean of FoGS, a commentary by the vice-president, Academic, and the like, combined with a report from the acting head of the Department of Political Science. At my insistence, the package included some rapidly compiled statistics (of the type shown in chapter 4), but I was told that I could speak only "from the floor." The acting head gave a spirited defence of his department and urged the senate to remove the suspension – but there was no motion on the floor at that meeting. Finally, a notice of motion was put forward by a female member of the Faculty of Arts, and for the next month the "sides" prepared their defences.

THE FoGS MEETING OF 10 OCTOBER 1995 AND THE DEAN'S STATEMENT

Before the senate meeting in October, the Graduate Council (an advisory committee to the dean of FoGS composed of faculty and graduate students, elected according to the proportion of faculty and graduate students in each faculty) met to vote on a motion to lift the suspension. The motion had been put forward by a member of the Faculty of Arts two weeks earlier, and in the interval politics had occupied everyone's attention. The motion was roundly defeated by a vote of forty-three to nine, with four abstentions.

Immediately before the vote, the dean of FoGS issued a statement in written as well as oral form. This lashed out at all his opponents, especially me, and made accusations against "white males." Because he attacked me so strongly, my bias should be kept in mind as I try to report this episode. I shall use his words to convey his message, but I am allowing myself footnotes where I believe his statements are inaccurate.

The dean began by observing that the decision to implement the suspension (which he acknowledged as his own, referring to it as "my" decision) had led to criticism, innuendo, and misinformation, and he stated without reservation that this had been "orchestrated by those in the Department and the Faculty of Arts" who opposed the Report and the suspension.[14] He warned that those who opposed him might "set back the causes of educational equity and academic freedom." He then provided his blueprint for the ideal university graduate program – a program in which students were "included" and were well supported intellectually, financially, and socially, and in which there was respect and tolerance: "Stereotypes on the basis of race, gender, age or other extraneous factors are not consistent with such a community."

He noted that complaints had initially been raised in 1992 and 1993. These, together with the department's autocritique based on questions to graduate students in 1994, the external reports, and finally the McEwen Report, were all consistent in showing that there was a problem. The acting head had admitted publicly there were problems, said the dean, and everybody in the department agreed that there were.[15] He went on at length to castigate the dean of arts and the members of the department who, he argued, had had input into the terms of reference and had accepted Ms McEwen as the investigator but now objected to the result. He asked if they would have objected "if the result had been the exoneration that they sought and expected."[16]

The dean defended McEwen's methods, arguing that she had been "scrupulously careful to follow due process provisions,"[17] and he explained that the suspension had been necessary because of the contents of the Report; because of the delay since complaints had first been raised and the lack of departmental response to these complaints; because of the seriousness of the complaints about educational equity, discrimination, and harassment; and because of the graduate program's weaknesses. He said he had imposed similiar penalties on other departments and "the only difference in this case was the publicity generated."[18] He then stated his belief that the publicity had been initiated by the dean of arts and the Department of Political Science in their press release of 29 July 1994, and he blamed them for "insisting that the report from the Enquiry be made public."[19] The dean similarly

castigated those who had characterized his behaviour and that of the
students as "McCarthyism" or "political correctness."

I noted in chapter 1 that the dean had taken a position on "white"
males. The passage I quoted there was from this document, and
because it is central to the debate, I shall repeat it here. He stated,
"Until relatively recently, Universities have been dominated by senior
white male faculty members. It is not surprising, but unacceptable, for
this group to seek to perpetuate its domination of our University." The
dean went on to applaud himself and his faculty for improving the
situation for women and minorities, and he warned that removal of
the suspension would inform students that their concerns were second-
ary to faculty concerns. Finally, he referred to "demographics" in his
attack on the motion to lift the suspension, implying that only "white"
males were of that persuasion.

THE SENATE MEETING, 18 OCTOBER 1995

Many months before these events occurred, I had committed myself
to being on another continent in October 1995 and was thus unable
to attend the next meeting of the senate, held on 18 October. From
Caracas I sent forth nagging faxes and phone calls, especially in
response to the public statement by the dean of FoGS, but I could not
engage in the day's tense round of discussions that led to an amazing
conclusion.

Leading up to this meeting, numerous interest groups had issued
bulletins and missives to the university senators. The president's office
had compiled its briefs, but so had the Department of Political Science,
the Graduate Student Society, and also twenty-nine graduate students
in the department. It was probably the last of these that carried the
day. Signed and delivered, the students' eloquent letter said that they
were deeply committed to fostering an environment sensitive to "issues
of race, gender, and to intellectual and epistomological pluralism." In
their view, the suspension did not contribute to these goals and in fact
created unnecessary impediments to implementing change. They spoke
of deep divisions between students and the need to rebuild the community. They called the suspension a "punishment" that affected not
only faculty but students.

Within two hours of the senate meeting, the dean of FoGS acceded
to pressure from many quarters and agreed to withdraw the ban on
graduate admissions. Amidst hissing and booing from graduate students in the galleries (even an effigy – though of what I never discovered – hung from the balcony), he made his announcement to the
senate. For all practical purposes, this was the end of the affair.

EPILOGUE

By way of epilogue, it should be noted that the president's handlers had to do some mending of public fences. For months after the apparent conclusion of the affair, a spate of admiring articles about him appeared in the *Vancouver Sun*, the *Globe and Mail*, and the UBC *Alumni Chronicle*, all of them playing down the affair. The president was quoted in the *Chronicle* as saying:

I think the report was flawed in many ways, but I don't think that's the substance of the issue. What was happening in the department, and what the department was doing about it was, in my view, the real substance of the issue. For others, the issue was the report itself and the approach used to develop it. They felt that the process of putting the report together did not allow for a fair presentation of views. Even if they are correct on the matter of process, my reaction was aimed at dealing with the substance of the issue – the challenge to academic freedom – not at dealing with due process or the process of the report. I think there was too much focus on the report, and not enough on the issues.[20]

This was said even though the president had earlier admitted that he had no information about the department beyond the Report. Thus was he prepared to use his powerful position to punish a group on the basis of his private beliefs. One must credit him with honesty, though he was clearly not concerned with due process.

Despite all these developments, some students were not prepared to drop the issue, and in the 1 March 1996 edition of the *Ubyssey*, the student who had transferred to another department after failing her comprehensives in political science was quoted as complaining that her application for a Social Sciences and Humanities Research Council grant had failed because political science faculty had not sent in letters of reference for her and because one letter that was sent (obtained, according to the newspaper, under Freedom of Information provisions) "delegitimized" her work. Department records diverged from this report, and requests for further information with an offer to investigate received no response from the dean of FOGS or the complainant. While the SSHRCC could not comment on any specific file, its officers said that no file is ever considered until and unless all letters of reference are included.

Both the Faculty of Arts and the Department of Political Science had meanwhile created committees to recommend new procedures for dealing with various student concerns. The faculty report, written by a committee that included persons with opposing viewpoints on the political science affair, was a model of cooperative deliberation. It focused on procedures for dealing with student complaints and was adopted by a general assembly in February 1996. Had it and the university's Equity Office been in place earlier, many of the problems might have been avoided. In future cases, both faculty and students would be obliged to act with more prudence.

The department deliberated over the next several months and delivered a departmental "Progress Report" in May 1996, as required under the agreement to lift the suspension. Some of the conditions which the department imposed on itself for supervising graduate students exceeded the requirements elsewhere in the university. Among the many issues was the concern to be both equitable and flexible. The head noted that the department had not earlier systematized its procedures to keep pace with the growth in graduate numbers. It now provided explicit conditions for any deviation from strict procedural equity between students. In addition to meeting the imposed conditions, the department made several recommendations to the dean of FOGS. Among these was the suggestion that the university undertake to create better tests for assessing language capacities and that it provide funds for remedial language training for students whose communication skills in English were deficient. Finally, and for the first time since the publication of the McEwen Report, the department as a whole went on record about its views:

Whereas the McEwen Report has been widely and justly condemned (by the Canadian Association of University Teachers, the B.C. Civil Liberties Association, in *The Advocate*, by the Heads of Departments in the UBC Arts Faculty, etc.) as a gross violation of due process, fairness, and logic, and whereas senior UBC administrators, with the notable exception of the Dean of Arts, have evaded a forthright declaration on the Report's flaws and inadequacies, we feel it is necessary to declare that our ongoing efforts to improve teaching and education in the Political Science Department predate the McEwen Report and in no way constitute an endorsement of its content or methodology.

The department head added: "I imagine my own feelings mirror those of many colleagues and quite a few graduate students – anger, dismay, frustration, exhaustion, and depression. And, yes, a feeling of disgust that my Department has been held to higher standards of forbearance and integrity than some of our most vocal critics." He spoke of being warned by the dean of FOGS and the associate deans of FOGS, as well as by administrators in the president's office, to maintain silence when students made misleading, offensive, or demeaning statements about the department. Such offences occurred with some frequency, he said, and "some critics have practised the intolerance, exclusivity, discrimination, and personal harassment which constituted the substance of most allegations against us."

Thus, the debate continues, with thrust and counterthrust. An article in the *Chronicle of Higher Education*, published on 24 May 1996, quoted the opposing views of two leading graduate students. One had referred to "a massive imbalance of power between graduate students and faculty," while the other had stated, "This dispute was portrayed early on as faculty versus student when, in fact, it pitted students against students." The *Chronicle's* article was headed "Wounds That Haven't Healed," and indeed one year after submission of the McEwen Report, the department was still in shock, as were many others who had dealt closely with the matter. Although the affair had been put to bed, it had not been laid to rest.

There is one further epilogue note. Two students, Ms Jones and Ms Keate, made formal complaints against members of the Department of Political Science to the B.C. Council of Human Rights. To the best of my knowledge as of June 1996, the council had not considered these. Naturally, no particulars can be discussed.

CHAPTER EIGHT

Text and Context

As I noted at the beginning of this narrative, no one defended racism and sexism, and no one wanted to be racist and sexist or to have colleagues so afflicted. This was never a debate over the legitimacy of racism and sexism. It was a debate over a process, a document, and judgments about racism and sexism in a university department. Nonetheless, and perhaps inevitably, the issues became clouded as the debate became more impassioned.

In debates on such sensitive issues it often happens that those who claim that their colleagues have transgressed sound "holier than thou"; those who claim that the labelling is unfair sound defensive, and they are in fact fearful of acquiring awful labels themselves. So fear, frustration, and anger are prominent features of debates such as the one that took place at the University of British Columbia in the summer and fall of 1995.

Imagine an advisory council to a dean, most of its members male and by the dean's definition "white," trying to vote independently after being told by the dean that negative votes would represent the attempt by "white" men to retain power and privilege; then add to the scenario a president's support for the dean's position. Imagine being a dean in another faculty where opinion was so sharply divided that no public stance would be tolerated by half of the faculty members. Imagine holding a minority opinion in a faculty where most members took the other side. Imagine two friends disagreeing over the Report, both of them obliged by their jobs and circumstances to be opinion leaders. These situations all actually occurred, and there were many other painful moments while the debate took place. I could find nothing salutary about this confrontation, and I have not seen any positive outcome from it. Months and months later, the bitterness remained like an acrid smell across the campus.

How shall we understand this event? Was it really about sexism and racism, or was it about something else that occasionally or intermittently linked up with issues of sex and race? Was it about power and privilege more generally, or only about the power and privilege of men who were "white," as Ms McEwen and the dean of FOGS argued? Why were people's passions so aroused? Why were reasonable academics and administrators so angry with one another?

One way of understanding the political science affair might be to read the texts and critically assess them on the basis of what was said, placing what was said in the immediate social context. This is what I propose to do in this chapter. Having so far described the texts, I shall now assess the central one. I shall consider the McEwen text on its own terms, as a document that says what it purports to say; and I shall consider the allegations within the context of a society that tolerates a fair degree of sexism and racism, and a university that has conflicting mandates for academic freedom and nonsexist, nonracist behaviour. I shall not attempt to answer the question of guilt, since my entire "take" on this is that no one can judge guilt on the basis of the information provided in the McEwen and other texts. But I shall try to consider what the allegations amount to at the end of the day if one takes them all at face value.

A very different approach would be to go beyond any particulars of the case. I move forward to that level of analysis in the concluding chapter, where I consider the case as an instance of social change, where what was said is viewed as a political manœuvre with objectives far beyond the categories identified in the McEwen text.

SEXISM

There were no reported cases of seduction, rape, sexual favours exchanged for grades or other misuse of privilege. This does not mean that sexism was absent, but it reduces the range of misbehaviours under consideration.

Inappropriate Socializing

Was there sexism in the form of uninvited flirtations, unwelcome forms of socializing, comments that involved gender inappropriately? The answer is "probably." There is probably sexism of this kind in every university department where there are both men and women. Unwanted flirtations probably occur everywhere. That does not excuse them, but it places the allegations in context. Hugging, breast touching, chatting up and asking for dates, commenting on appearance, looking (and sometimes not looking) can all be offensive behaviour, and they are the very stuff of basic, crude sexism. They trivialize women by reducing them to their physical parts, and this is unpardonable, especially in a university department.

If Ms McEwen had investigated all those allegations that could be followed up, and if she had then eliminated those for which a reasonable alternative interpretation or contrary information existed, she would have had a greater positive impact. Unfortunately, she threw allegations that could appropriately be identified as having to do with sexism together with some that could more appropriately be considered curriculum concerns. By way of justification, she advanced the thesis that everything was part and parcel of sexism and racism; but the indiscriminate mixture muddled rather than clarified the issues. She also included allegations that had already been refuted by the supposed victims (for example, that the secretarial staff were harrassed by male faculty) and allegations for which reasonable alternative explanations had already been provided. A prime example of the latter was the complaint against the faculty member who had offered a female student the use of an overnight bedroom during an evening seminar at his home. He had already stated – well before McEwen's appointment – that his offer had been made in good faith to the student, who resided on Vancouver Island and had a tight ferry schedule; moreover, he said that his wife had been present when he made the offer.

Nevertheless, if we remove the excess baggage, there would still remain allegations of crude and stupid comments and behaviour by male faculty. One is inclined to believe that these incidents occurred simply because they do occur in virtually every organization and every sphere of women's lives. Even so, in an investigative report, we should have been provided with the responses from faculty members to each specific charge, and we should have been informed about the immediate context. Evidence should have been sought wherever possible. Arriving at judgments without such information is simply unfair. It was the injustice of the process that turned me against McEwen's report rather than my own beliefs about whether or not these (or any other) men could have behaved in such ways.

"Chilly Climate" Issues

Whereas trivializing women by treating them as pets or playthings is an obvious form of sexism, "chilly climate" claims are more subtle. They consist of arguments that women are marginalized when professors (male or female) ignore or dismiss their contribution while welcoming the participation of male students in intellectual discussions.

This kind of behaviour is often unconscious on the part of faculty and amounts to systemic and unintended discrimination. However, in the text as presented, "chilly climate" issues were not separately discussed. There were comments or observations reported that might – but also might not – be pertinent, and I have included them in other sections.

One clearly belongs here, though. It involves the cut and thrust of academic debate. Academic discussions frequently engage several speakers at once and in competition, and women do have a complaint when men – especially those with louder voices or habits of "taking over" events – speak over them. Men might similarly complain that sometimes women "take charge" and leave them speechless. Complaints of this type are part and parcel of "chilly climates," but unless one were to watch the interactions in class and in academic debates for some time, one really could not say that any particular instance of someone "speaking over" others was proof of sexism. A somewhat sceptical outsider might also ask why the women let it happen. Women do have voices as well as brains, and objecting once or twice would probably alter the dynamics of such a debate. This would be especially true where women are in the majority, as they were in most political science classes. However, let us assume that there were male professors who were insensitive to the domination of debate by assertive male students. This is a "chilly climate" issue, and female students caught in such a situation would have had cause to complain.

As with the accusations of unwanted flirtation, many of the allegations about unequal treatment needed context, and faculty should have been given a chance to respond to specific claims. If, for example, only women's names were ever omitted from conference programs or departmental announcements of award winners, the claims of discrimination in two cases described in the Report would have been entirely justified. But McEwen did not examine a representative array of programs and announcements to test the allegation, so the reader cannot judge whether these incidents represesented gender-neutral negligence or genuine discrimination.

Discriminatory Treatment of Women

One form of discrimination would consist of grading and awards practices that were different for men and women; as was seen from the data I presented in chapter 4, there was no evidence of grading differences, and women were proportionately represented among the nominations for awards. The accusation that there was overt discrimination in the awards of the Social Sciences and Humanities Research Council of Canada was demonstrably untrue: the same ranking pertained as for university fellowships, and the data for university fellowships were made public by the university.

The student survey showed that men received more grant income than women (true across the university as well as in this department). This might indicate discrimination, but to test this thesis one would have to eliminate (or hold constant) other potential explanations. For example, MA students receive less than PhD students in every program. Since fewer women are in PhD programs, women's average income from grants would be lower if there were no discrimination by sex. In this department, there were two men to each woman in the PhD program, so one would expect that any measures that failed to distinguish between the MA and PhD levels would show men overall as receiving higher grant funding. As well, part-time students have less access to funds than full-time students. Slightly more women then men were part-time students, and that would have influenced the grant distribution. In view of these facts, the larger amount of grant income received by men is not in itself proof of discrimination.

The charge that large numbers of women were fleeing the PhD program was also dealt with in chapter 4 and shown to be invalid. As indicated by the data (which McEwen cited only partially), three women and three men had failed comprehensives between 1970 and 1995; four women and fifteen men had voluntarily withdrawn; and three women and one man had withdrawn in order to transfer to other universities or programs, or for medical reasons.

While discrimination is more easily identified in measurable units such as grants, it also exists in classroom behaviour that diminishes women and downgrades their contribution. There were allegations of this kind, but almost all of them were ambiguous. For many, the context had to be known in order to assess the claim. For others, a claim was made but its implications were unclear. Some had to do with likes and dislikes but were not self-evidently related to discrimination on the basis of sex.

Under the heading "Mentoring and Thesis Supervision" there was one complaint by a female student about a female faculty member's reaction to the student's proposal to change thesis topics, and McEwen noted that the student characterized the teacher as "sexist." From the way this incident was recorded in the Report, it was simply incomprehensible. The reader had no context, no idea why the professor might have expressed hostility (assuming this occurred as reported) and was left with nothing more than a gossipy account of a conflict between a supervisor and a student. Was this supposed to indicate sexism between two women?

There were several allegations in the section "The Graduate Program" that should have been investigated. The "Jewish female" who failed comprehensives blamed her failure on a faculty member who mentored a "male of colour" but refused to mentor her. This story was difficult to untangle because the student's religious affiliation did not appear to have anything to do with the complaint, and it was equally irrelevant that the other student was "of colour." What the reader needed to know was whether the faculty member was unfair (or whether the rules for scheduling comprehensives were systemically unfair) to a woman who had recently given birth and had limited time for study.

Under the title "Classroom Environment Issues and Evaluation of Students," there were numerous allegations about "white male professors" who did many unsavoury things. Several of these allegations were insufficiently precise for the reader to reach any reasonable judgment about whether racism or sexism was the appropriate allegation (irrespective of whether the event actually occurred). One example is that of the professor who failed to reprimand one student yet silenced another. As with so many of the allegations, the context is not described. A professor might choose not to silence a student in the interests of open discussion, yet might silence a particular student who was rude or disruptive; similarly, the professor might find some comments relevant and others irrelevant. Further, the meaning of "silencing" is not self-evident. Allegations of this kind should have been put to the professors against whom they were lodged, and their responses should have been included so that the reader could judge whether the behaviour had anything to do with sexism or racism.

It will be recalled that one of the allegations was that faculty failed to articulate the criteria for evaluating classroom participation, "thus disadvantaging those students who typically do not enjoy the same access to it, namely the women and students of colour." But McEwen did not offer any enlightenment about why these students would be disadvantaged by this practice. There may well have been a problem in the department about the articulation of criteria – the department members have conceded as much, and they had started to address it in a massive overhaul of the PhD program many months before McEwen submitted her report – but it is not self-evident that this organizational failure was systemically (I presume) tied to sexism and racism. The same would be true for the allegations about marking procedures and grades for class participation.

One or more students alleged stereotyping, but the Report gave only the accusation. Evidence at best consisted of subjective interpretation.

In what way was a student stereotyped? And on what basis did she/
he read an outcome (low grades, lack of award) as stereotyping? Given
the hard data available on distribution of grades and awards, did
McEwen assess the reasonableness of these claims?

Homophobic behaviour was implied in the case of the professor who
was accused of refusing to mark an essay by a female lesbian undergraduate – an essay which, according to the student challenged heterosexual assumptions. Here again, the context is crucial, and as usual,
no contextual information is provided. Did the professor assign topics?
Was the course's subject matter such that an essay on this topic would
have been relevant? Was the professor aware that the student was
lesbian, and was that relevant?

Some of the allegations suggest what one might call equal-
opportunity or gender-free rudeness. Faculty were accused of showing
insensitivity, ignorance, or outright rudeness towards students, and a
judge should certainly be concerned about that, whether or not the
behaviour was sexist or racist. But since McEwen did not distinguish
between allegations of rudeness and those about sexism and racism,
the reader is left with insufficient contextual information to make the
distinctions.

Other allegations referred to faculty behaviour that was sharp or
indicated impatience or disbelief, yet that might on occasion have been
warranted. What is one to say, for example, about the student who
requested the favour of audit status, arrived late to the class, and then
complained of a "hostile and authoritarian response" when the professor failed to appreciate her tardiness? And in what way was this
indicative of sexism?

Overt Antifeminism

More precise was the allegation that (one or more?) professors
attacked the concept of "chilly climate" and feminist theory,
denounced feminists in the classroom, and refused to use gender-
inclusive language. These are serious allegations, and, if they are true,
they do indicate at the very least a lack of understanding of feminism.
It is a lack of understanding that should not exist in a university
department, especially in a department such as political science that is
engaged in studies of contemporary society.

Unfortunately, these allegations in the McEwen Report were not
investigated. We do not know whether one professor or more expressed
hostility, or whether the attacks consisted of responses to feminism or
were academic rebuttals of any specific feminist argument. I am
inclined to keep this particular set of charges on the counter as "yet

to be investigated" and as being potentially indicative of sexism (whether or not pervasive).

Female Faculty

There was no contest on this: the department acknowledged its failure to attract and keep female faculty over previous years. However, it pointed to its recent hiring record (four out of five new faculty were female) to show that change was underway.

McEwen claimed that female faculty members felt excluded and unfairly treated by their male colleagues, but she offered no evidence. In September 1995, one of the department's untenured female professors stood up in a public audience to encourage members of the Faculty of Arts to vote in favour of a motion to lift the suspension on graduate admissions. She argued: there is sexism in this department; there was sexism in the last department I worked in, and one before that, and in every one where I have studied. We need to combat sexism, and I think this department is trying to do that. I also think punishment is not the way to change people, and this punishing situation hurts women faculty members as much as men.

It took a great deal of courage for her to deliver that message in the emotionally charged atmosphere of that assembly.

RACISM

Rudeness and "apparently racist comments" are not reasonable behaviour in a classroom and should not be condoned. However, rudeness may have diverse attributes according to perception, and a "racist comment" may not be understood as such by all who hear it. A fair judge confronted with the information that a professor had penalized a student for arriving late to class would need considerably more contextual information before concluding that the professor was acting in a racist or sexist way. Many of the accusations were of this kind, and while McEwen argued that the accumulation of them was itself sufficient evidence, I do not think that such an argument has justice on its side.

It is not impossible to investigate cases such as these. An investigation could have determined whether the professor in question ever penalized men or non-Caucasians, whether other students had witnessed the event and how they interpreted it, and whether other students considered that the professor was acting within his rights (students should not arrive late for class) or was acting in an unnecessarily brusque way.

Racism and Curriculum

One complaint was that the faculty were ethnocentric and that their theoretical perspectives were Western. While this referred mostly to "white" males, one of the complaints referred to a "female professor of colour" who did not demonstrate sufficient breadth in a course on "Women and Development."

It was certainly the case that most faculty members were products of American universities. Although theoretical perspectives had changed and multiplied since they were students, mainstream American theories were still less concerned with class divisions and economic power than the British and European versions were. Feminist theories had penetrated political science as a discipline, but they were not featured in this department. More critical theories of the capitalist state – neo-Marxist or Gramscian approaches, for example – were taught in Canadian universities but no one at UBC specialized in teaching these approaches. On the other hand, several of this department's members were renowned for their expertise on Canadian constitutional issues and for sophisticated studies of Canadian voting patterns, and others had a strong record of research in European and other countries. If students found the range of theoretical perspectives too limited, that was a matter of concern, but was it related to the twin isms?

There is no single theoretical perspective that would uniquely encompass non-Western ways of thinking in the way that feminism encompasses non-male approaches to the world. One might – and most Western-trained social scientists would – apply theoretical perspectives of the Western world to the non-Western world. Thus, theories of development and underdevelopment, neo-Marxist theories, political economy, postmodernism, feminism, and cultural studies, all of which are critical of Western imperialism, are part of the usual canon of Western universities and were, for the most part, created in them.

If the criticism of faculty inattention to non-Western ways of thinking was intended to imply that insufficient attention was given to critical theories, the evidence appears to support the claim; but if it was other than this, the complainants needed to specify which particular theoretical traditions were accessible and could reasonably be included in a Canadian curriculum. It would be unjust to say that because faculty failed to include critical perspectives, they were racists; although the complaint that they were too immersed in American theories implied intellectual narrowness, it was not evidence of racism.

Theoretical approaches aside, possibly the intention was to argue that the curriculum omitted empirical studies of other cultures. On the face of it this seems unlikely, since the faculty's research interests included studies on India, China, Japan, and parts of Africa, though the majority of faculty members concentrated on Canada, the United States, and various states of Europe. In the previous half-dozen years the faculty had lost a couple of high-profile specialists in Asian studies and had not yet replaced them at the time of the memoranda (because of insufficient funding). These research interests suggest no discriminatory attitudes towards these cultures and regions. Another allegation in this set was that the advertised capacities of the department were false with reference to its strength in Asian studies. As just noted, the department had lost strength in this field. If it was advertising strengths it no longer had, then it deserved the complaint. But, again, this does not add up to racism. This allegation was dealt with in the department head's response in 1992, and it could have been investigated by reading the advertisements.

The allegation that referred to a female professor "of colour" who failed to include sufficient Third World feminist writers in her course materials could easily be reversed, and the complainant could be called "racist" for pointing to a "woman of colour." The complaint was problematic as reported by McEwen, since the reader is given no idea what the course was about, whether or not it had some feminist writers, whether there were other outstanding and relevant writers who could have been included, and so on. One must ask: Was the student aware of other feminist writers who could have been included? Had she/he spoken to the professor about this perceived lack of balance? Was the professor given the opportunity to respond and, if appropriate, to add those writers to the course materials? The reader is offered no answers to such questions but is simply told, as if it were a conclusion, that the student regarded the course as "not enlightening" and "just a perpetuation of stereotypes."

In the allegations made before the McEwen Report and repeated there, a student used the term "racism" in reference to a professor who had informed her that her preferred thesis topic was "impossible to handle." To sustain such a charge, one would have to suppose that professors do not regularly tell a large number of students of every skin colour and both sexes that their choice of topics is inappropriate, not do-able (the usual phrase), or beyond the capacity of these students at this stage of their studies. Since we know that such advice is normal, that virtually every student who ever took a PhD has been told this at least once, the charge cannot be left on the books. The same is true of the student who charged a professor with sexism when he advised her to take an undergraduate course by way of preparation for study at a higher level on the subject. Again, this is normal (and usually good) advice. If taken, it saves the student many hours of wasted effort learning basic material.

Some of the allegations, such as the one above, seem trivial to anyone who has taught students and tried to find ways of helping them master preliminary material before embarking on a thesis. Others, however, were weighty; an example is an Afro-American or African student who was treated shabbily by a professor in a classroom exchange. She asked a serious question about the theory under discussion, and he responded by talking about Africans. His response was perceived – and if it was accurately reported, I have to say I would also perceive it – as condescending. This was not a trivial allegation. It is most regrettable that it was not investigated seriously, and if found to have occurred as described (there were other students who must have been witnesses), the professor should most certainly have been identified and been obliged to answer for his rudeness.

Ms McEwen included as evidence of racism recommendations by faculty to students whose first language was not English that they take steps to improve their communication skills. The university instructs in the English language, and political science is a subject that requires fluency and not merely literacy in the language of instruction. Degrees granted are supposed to indicate that mastery of the subject in the language of instruction has taken place. In what way, then, are faculty racist when they make suggestions for improvement in language skills? At least one complaint on this score referred to the fact that the best papers were produced by "white males" and that professors recommended to others that they read the best papers. The skin colours and genders, when associated in such clear-cut ways with differences in communication skills, undoubtedly led to tensions, but the professors who expected skills in the language of instruction were not responsible for differences in skills and their distribution.

Finally, there were various allegations in which the complainants were referred to as Jewish. Some of these incidents seem to have involved direct and unambiguous rudeness with definite sexist and racist overtones – for instance, the alleged observation that feminism is a "Jewish-American Princess conspiracy." That complaint should have been investigated further. So should the complaint of the Jewish woman who said she had not been allowed an exemption from class on a Jewish holy day. But as I noted in an earlier chapter, one must wonder why there is this emphasis on the Jewish religion and not on any other. What, for example, is one to make of the case of the "white Jewish female MA student" who complained of a professor's sexist remarks? In this allegation, the only two relevant terms are "female" and "student," yet the implication is that the professor is anti-Semitic as well as sexist. When such implications are included (as they are throughout the text), a reader begins to wonder who is the more racist – the faculty member against whom the allegation is made or the investigator who implies a dimension of racism that is not self-evidently relevant to the charge.

CURRICULUM AND PROGRAM ORGANIZATION

There were three problems acknowledged by the faculty in the Department of Political Science. One was that they had expanded their graduate programs too rapidly and had too many students relative to faculty resources, student funding, and office space. A second was that the PhD program was not well organized; this had been noted by the external reviewers, and long before the McEwen inquiry was underway the department had begun an overhaul of procedures. The third was that the department did not have someone who was an expert in feminist theory. After reading the departmental review, the faculty agreed to give this highest priority for hiring when next they were able to recruit new members. Their vote on this was in the public record and was forwarded to both deans and, later, to McEwen. The question for McEwen, then, was not whether the program had organizational deficiencies but whether any of the deficiencies were related to or caused by sexism or racism. On the face of it, only the third appeared to be related to sexism, and the department had already acknowledged this deficiency and had proposed the solution before McEwen's investigation began.

The memoranda submitted by the students made numerous allegations about the curriculum. Some of these charges were addressed by the department head in letters of response, some of the strongest being refuted on factual or statistical grounds, but it was clear that students and faculty were not on the same wavelength. McEwen's attempt to describe this divergence in her cruel depiction of the faculty culture in contrast to student culture did at least oblige faculty to recognize the gulf between their versions of the scholarly enterprise and that of the graduate students. The gulf was by no means peculiar to this department at this university. Unfortunately, McEwen increased the gulf by failing to listen to advice that would have informed her about the nature of graduate studies in the social sciences. Although expected to consult with named academic advisers, she refused to do so. The consequence was, as expressed by one of the faculty members,

that Ms. McEwen was incapable of distinguishing ordinary academic procedure from evidence of racism/sexism. In my case, a complaint in a letter made anonymous by the Administration alleged that in a graduate seminar in 1991 I granted essay extensions to two male students. Indeed I did; one for medical reasons and the other to my TA [teaching assistant] who was helping me mark exams for a course of 150 students. I told Ms. McEwen that I normally grant extensions for reasons such as these, and do so for women as often as for men. I also told her that in the seminar in question, no woman student had requested an extension. The inference of favouritism in the allegation was thus invalid on both empirical and logical grounds. Nevertheless, Ms. McEwen used the original allegation as part of the "evidence" to substantiate her claim that there is indeed a basis for the overall allegation of "pervasive racism and sexism" in the Department.[1]

Rebuttals of this kind were numerous. Previous chapters have referred to several rebuttals of specific claims where the accused were identified or identified themselves. Quite apart from the substance of the claims and rebuttals, what strikes one most forcefully is the divergence of perspective. The faculty member quoted above may have been correct, but what mattered to the student was not truth: it was her perception. McEwen accepted perceptions as facts, and consequently the professor's rebuttal became irrelevant.

Information that would have been useful might have included an appraisal of the social sciences. In these disciplines, faculty must discuss contemporary issues – delicate and emotion-laden issues – in the classroom. Students in chemistry have no reason to take personal offence at the description of the properties of a chemical reaction, but in the social sciences virtually every topic is susceptible to interpretation and miscommunication.

Some part of the issues faced in this debate, then, were caused by ignorance and misinformation, and some by a genuine difference in perception and understanding; but there were some allegations that could not be explained as readily as the one noted in the above quotation, and not everything in the Report could be reduced to Ms McEwen's failure to grasp how graduate education takes place.

One of the difficulties here was that the stated allegations were often tangential to what was actually being said. For instance, the students appeared to complain about what was said in class, and this gave rise to many defences of academic freedom. But reading between the lines, it appears that the students were not complaining about radical views expressed in the context of lectures; they were complaining about the deficiency of them, about the sheer lack of inspiration in their lectures. Some of the complaints seemed to be that at the end of the day the students did not feel challenged; they remained uninformed about too much. One senses, reading the seemingly trite complaints, that the students were implying that they found their teachers to be smug, overbearing, out-of-date, and unimaginative. They attributed these traits to the fact that the teachers were male and "white." Then others joined the chorus, and all "white men" became targets. But perhaps I read in too much here; the problem is that so little of the text is really about what it says it is about, and one goes in search of other possibilities.

GENERAL OBSERVATIONS ON THE TEXT

When all the differences in assumptions and expectations are considered and when all the disputes about the nature of the alleged crimes and appropriate moral codes are taken into account, have we ended up with genuine villains and certain victims? This is really the nub of it, isn't it? There is no doubt that some of the reported behaviour stank – the unwelcome hugs and the eyeballing of women are outstanding examples – and that some students wanted to learn something that these faculty members could not teach. But do these add up to crimes worthy of the noise this event generated?

The organization of the text of the Report was itself a problem. Similar allegations (and apparently by the same individual) were stated or restated under different headings. What appeared under "Inappropriate Socializing" and "Faculty/Student Interactions" or "Classroom Environment" had no obvious distinctions. Claims of sexism were frequently joined to claims of racism or were phrased in such a way that one was not sure whether religious affiliation was integral to the complaint.

Complaints about the curriculum were phrased as complaints about sexism or racism, whether or not the linkage was self-evident. One such complaint was that the curriculum was "male and white." Another, noted throughout the text, was that the word "aggressive" even when meaning "energetic" was male in gender. If a curriculum can be intrinsically "male and white," then the entire intellectual world is subject to a similar charge. This is indeed the argument of those who want to overthrow patriarchy. For them, it is not sufficient to add feminist theory and female writers; we have to debunk and discard all the theory already on the books which, in their view, blindly expresses the perspectives of men and addresses men.

One could understand the complaint if it referred to a text that treated women or any others as inferior, such as various parts of Shakespeare, Plato, and Marx. But one wonders whether other works by European or American men would necessarily be included: experiments in the natural or medical sciences, for example, or Francis Bacon talking about the rules of induction and deduction, or Albert Camus on existentialism. In a sense, surely, everything that has ever been produced – from Aristotle to Jane Austen, from Beethoven to a modern Chinese opera or Madonna – embodies something of its author's identity, so sex (or at least gender) and ethnicity (or at least regional cultures) might affect the outcome. Still, to label the entire canon in a subject "male and white" would suggest that that is all there is to it.

On the other hand, if women and men – or most women and men – receive, process, and use information in different ways, then any system that favours one way will be *systemically* biased against the other. Thus the claim, reported several times in the Report, that the curriculum was "male and white" would have some meaning. But we do not have the necessary information to decide whether this is true; and if it were true, it would necessarily also be true of every curriculum everywhere. For all its sins, political science does not seem large enough to carry the whole burden of history.

One has to consider the assumptions of the statement I have just made, for obviously I am a product of an educational system that postulates the objective existence of "truth" independent of my versions of it. Thus can I say that we need more information to determine truth: I cannot assume either that no truth exists or that my truth is as good as any other truth. But suppose we sought agreement rather than truth, thus acceding to the postmodernist or at least Kuhnsian notion of how science determines its validity. In that case, would we not suppose that the number of people agreeing that they saw the same thing is crucial? But in this affair, we did not know how many students actually complained on various occasions or how many actually believed the department to be sexist and racist. Five spoke on behalf of twelve, and then on behalf of eighteen, and maybe there were dozens who complained to McEwen; but just as likely there were never more than five or six. There were twenty-nine who argued otherwise and signed their names. So if consensus rather than "objective evidence" is to be the test, the few anonymous are less persuasive than the named many. (I hasten to add that I do not subscribe to this position; I simply point it out as one way of considering the problem.)

One might argue that numbers are irrelevant, that one unhappy student is sufficient to justify an investigation. Well, perhaps, but it would be difficult to find a department in a university in which there is not one disgruntled student – and, more likely, at least half a dozen. If five were unhappy and twenty-nine satisfied, this would indicate that the problems – whatever they were – were not universal. Since we are dealing almost entirely with subjective accounts, with perceptions and allegations for which there is no objective evidence, we are obliged to make a decision right at the start about the credibility (no other term makes sense in this context) of the five who complained. Yet we have no evidence to test their credibility, and McEwen made no attempt to do so.

Two issues remain about the particulars of this event. Firstly, if all "white" males are sexist and racist, or if "white" society more generally is patriarchal, imperialistic, sexist, racist, and authoritarian, then in what respects would the political science department be worthy of singling out for punishment if it displayed sexist and racist behaviour? This is a serious question, as the analysis suggested in the final chapter will indicate, because if this department is regarded merely as an instance of something that pervades the whole society, then the punishment was symbolic. The department was being used as a negative model for others, or perhaps as a testing ground for ideas and strategies in a larger battle. If, on the other hand, the department was deviant in ways uncharacteristic of society at large (which would be consistent with the penalties imposed on it), why were the charges framed in terms of "white" males, and why was the defence of the penalty stated in terms of the proclivity of "white" males to defend their privileges?

The second issue concerns the student complainants. In considering the context and the power struggles endemic to North American and other university campuses, and in sceptically considering the charges as laid out by McEwen, I may appear to be indifferent to the pain these individuals say they have experienced. As a women who has survived a quarter century on the faculty, I have experienced my share of sexist behaviour, so the nature of the complaints is familiar to me and I do not doubt that there are hurt feelings. Chilly climates are real, and faculty and students alike must become conscious of their existence and their ill effects; I do not condone them, though I think they are more likely to be eradicated by persuasion than by punishment. My disagreement with the course of events in the Department of Political Science is not rooted in a lack of sympathy for the students but in my belief that all accused persons have the right to respond to complaints of this (or any other) kind. I do not accept the view adopted by McEwen and others that persons are guilty of serious sins – sexism and racism – because someone experiences their behaviour in a negative way.

There probably was insufficient listening on the part of faculty in response to the first and second memoranda, though since both were anonymous and the accused were unnamed, and since the head of the department did attempt to bring the "chilly climate" issues to the attention of faculty and made genuine efforts to reorganize the PhD program, I think that the persistent complaint about unresponsiveness was substantially overstated. Had the head known who the complainants were, he would have been able to bring the parties together and discuss the problems openly. That, clearly, was what was needed. Indeed, Ms McEwen said, in connection with the human rights cases still pending, that what was needed was "for the respondents to simply 'listen' to what the complainants are saying" (130). With respect to the "big bad black bitch" complaint, this was dealt with by the Sexual Harassment Policy Office, and apologies were sincerely given by the professor and (twice) by the department head.

When recording the complaints, Ms McEwen said that faculty "refused to accept, at face value, the student's stated experience." She went on: "In other words, the faculty refused to acknowledge – regardless of his/her own views – that a student may have experienced hurt and discrimination because of the way that she/he was being treated" (110). This is a problematic charge in light of the rest of this document. If the stated experience was entirely subjective and there was no external corroboration, and if the context and other information or evidence was contrary to the student's interpretation, would Ms McEwen have respectfully listened to the rebuttal and weighed the alternatives? Was it conceivable that in some instances the students' interpretations were fair but that in others the faculty members were not the culprits they were alleged to be? McEwen's statement implies that she refused to accept at face value, or any other value, the professors' experience. Neither she nor the faculty were listening, apparently, and their mutual deafness was a disservice to the students, whose complaints should have been taken seriously rather than merely literally and "at face value."

Finally, I, like others caught up in this affair, have tried to decide whether the list of allegations given in the McEwen Report and the earlier memos constitutes proof of sexism or racism in the department. At the end of the day, I do not know, and I do not see how anyone can know, on the basis of what is in front of us, whether this department was or was not guilty – and if it was guilty, precisely what was the nature of the crime. For me, the problem is not a disbelief in sexism or racism but the paucity of evidence, reasoned argument, and fair treatment of all individuals involved – in short, the lack of justice in the investigation.

As a faculty member trained in the Western rationalist tradition, I read the Report with growing incredulity. Where was the evidence? Where were the facts? Some of the allegations seemed trivial even if true, and the attacks on the curriculum seemed to have nothing to do with sexism or racism. Some were about universal problems but were not shown to be particularly evident in this single department. But clearly the writer of the Report, many of the complainants, and perhaps many other people too, used different yardsticks to judge the Report. In the concluding chapter, I propose to address these diverse understandings of events such as (but no longer restricted to) the political science affair at UBC.

CHAPTER NINE

Sweetness and Light?

Ms McEwen never entered the fray on the subject of postmodernism, and there is no reason to suppose that she was intellectually engaged by such theories. But the text she produced had a popular postmodernist stance to it. It never argued its case, it produced no evidence, and she stated that evidence was not required because the allegations were enough to demonstrate the case for her. It made no claims to truth – indeed, she explicitly informed readers that it mattered not whether the claims were true; it was enough that the complainants believed them to be true. It rested, finally, on a political position: that the department under study consisted mainly of "white" men and that "white" men were corrupt.

Her text was disjunctive with the Western rationalist tradition, but it was similar to texts and arguments being mounted in universities and colleges throughout the Western world. Current struggles over control of the curriculum, cultural diversity, meritocracy and egalitarianism, and the power associated with knowledge are widespread, and both the positions adopted at UBC and the modes of presentation have their counterparts in similar events elsewhere. The Victorians thought that the objective of a university was to inculcate philosophical habits of mind and that the objective of culture was to develop a harmonious match of goodness and intellect. The late twentieth century, by contrast, is struggling noisily with incompatible philosophies and values.

INCLUSIVENESS VS MERITOCRACY

Universities in the late twentieth century do not turn away students because of their sex, their ethnic or class origins, their religion, or their sexual orientation. Admissions may thus seem to be equitable and inclusive. However, students must meet certain academic standards, and once admitted they compete for grades, scholarships, other awards, and graduate status. In a world where admission to a university and eventual graduation from it are requisites for virtually any non-manual occupation, these meritocratic principles are barriers for those who are unable to meet the standards. This might be acceptable if the standards were judged to be entirely fair, but not all persons or groups accept them as such; some argue that the standards embody obstacles on such grounds as sex and ethnicity.

The standards are based on the assumption that individuals, not groups, are the basic units of society. Meritocracy by its nature treats persons as individuals; thus, a woman or a member of a minority ethnic group might rise to a position of prominence, but this would not necessarily alter the opportunities for other women or other members of the same ethnic group. While it is generally conceded that, in times past, group cultures may have influenced individual performance and that systemic or direct discrimination against groups may have influenced individual opportunities and rewards, meritocratic systems are defended as superior to alternatives such as quotas and the allocation of positions by group characteristics. Their superiority is claimed on grounds somewhat akin to Churchill's grounds in favour of democracy – that it is the worst possible system except for all the others.

Meritocracy, however, is not favoured by the numerous groups in Western society whose objective is to move their entire membership forward, using universities as the instruments for this group mobility. The only way these groups could ascend mobility ladders as groups would be by overturning the meritocracy principle and the standards on which that meritocracy is based. Thus, necessarily, the curriculum and the evaluation system would be targets for these groups. As well, the groups might demand group rights – for example, quotas and entitlements to certain proportions of graduate or professional school admissions, and of faculty and administrative positions.[1]

In this vein, then, the argument is mounted that even where students are a heterogeneous population, the curriculum remains Eurocentric and embedded in the Western rationalist tradition and is thus discriminatory against non-Europeans from more oral, less rationalistic cultural traditions. A gender-based group might argue that men reason in different ways from women and that reliance on the Western rationalist tradition therefore discriminates in a systemic way against women. Taking such positions, groups argue that the university is not inclusive, even where it allows anyone with the right grades to enter, unless it makes allowance for all possible differences between groups. This is the essence of identity politics.

At a point beyond the generalizations and abstractions of inclusive-ness and meritocracy are real teaching situations with real faculty and students.[2] A television host once rather pompously told me, on screen, that a subject was a subject was a subject: everyone, irrespective of sex, age, ethnicity, or religion, should be taught the same curriculum. This sounds fine to someone who has never stood in front of a class in the social sciences or humanities. A twenty-year-old single male and a forty-year-old female parent hear, see, and think differently, and their needs diverge. Should we ignore these differences and set the curricu-lum according to the perceptions of the fifty-year-old male who teaches the course? Add ethnicity and religion to the mix, also diverse sexual orientations and physical capacities, and the answer is no, we can no longer teach these courses as if the learners were homogeneous or their diversity was irrelevant.

But if we try to accommodate all divergence, we cannot provide a standard curriculum, and thus by striving for inclusiveness we jettison equality. Further, if the standards are related to something beyond any one class – entry to professional schools, for example – then conces-sions to diversity could diminish opportunities for the very people being protected by group identities and group demands.

Human rights codes now prohibit discrimination of kinds not even considered in past decades. A student demands exemption from a requirement in a performance course because it would involve spend-ing time on stage on a Sunday: forbidden by her religion. As noted in the complaints to McEwen, another student claims exemption because her religion forbids her to use public transportation on a particular day. A third student has to miss classes not so much because of a death in the family as because in her culture the death – which occurred some time previously – must be mourned for a specified length of time that severely cuts into her studies.

The university cannot ignore these claims in the 1990s, nor can it solve them by merely publishing requirements for courses if the requirements in any way discriminate against individuals because of ethnic, religious, or sexual orientation. Most universities – UBC included – have responded to social change by instituting human rights policies to address sexual harassment and discrimination on campus. They have employed counsellers and experts of various per-suasions to improve the teaching and learning environment for all students. But they are doing this in a context of shrinking budgets for the academic establishment. A cynical scholar observes, "Universities will become places where you feel good, but you won't be able to learn anything."

In these circumstances, what curriculum would be valid? What kind of information, what sort of knowledge, what canon or tradition could anglophone Canadian universities teach that would meet the needs of this diverse population? What now is a liberal education? How can we redefine the university in the midst of opposing directives?

Challenges to the curriculum are preludes to challenges to the evaluation systems. Faculty are urged to concern themselves with inclusiveness when marking students. The model of student as customer is radically different from that of student as trainee; both may be appropriate to learning, but the second gives faculty a right to determine or at least influence what is learned. The student-as-customer model might avoid the presumptions of faculty, but students might then lose the opportunity to learn challenging material or material that would be most useful to their life objectives. Still, that might be an acceptable trade-off for students, the defenders of the Western canon notwithstanding.

The student-as-customer model, however, leads one to question the point of evaluations, and there are already voices in favour of erasing failing grades from transcripts. Finally, the logical inference is that if faculty are no longer willing to insist on the value of the "great books" or whatever canon is their subject, and if they see themselves as reference librarians rather than teachers, on what grounds could one justify their evaluation of students?

POWER AND CONFLICT

When university degrees were rare and unnecessary for success in the world, when all that really counted in most fields was wealth or the ruthlessness required to gain wealth, the enmity of the people was reserved for the owners of the means of production (or of land or whatever was then valuable). But as knowledge became the source of power, inevitably it attracted the enmity of those barred from its attainment.

What is the power so envied, so possessed? For the professoriate as a group, it consists of the right to determine the curriculum – the agenda of the university. To determine the curriculum is also to exert a major influence on society's intellectual and cultural agenda: what is researched and what is not; where the intellectual resources are put; which fads, fashions, and topics are "in" and "out"; which novels, poems, and works of art; and what ideas oil the social machinery for the educated class. These ideas are never restricted to intellectual and artistic discussion; they have impact throughout the society, pushing some things away and pulling others closer to the nub. Economic and political power grow out of knowledge, and those who are the high priests of the knowledge institution share in the economic and political power of their time.

Universities and colleges as a group are major employers in all Western societies. They are far from the influential but small institutions that fed knowledge to a hand-picked student body in the last century or even prior to 1945. Although they do not themselves have political decision-making power and although they are not major economic powers in their own right, nonetheless they do exert a powerful influence on decision makers and on students who will become decision makers. Further, they engage in research that is occasionally of great moment to a field, an industry, a society, and through that they are powerful institutions.

For the individual, the power of knowledge involves not only the right to speak on a range of specialized topics as an expert but also the privilege of being listened to on a wide range of other topics as "an educated person." It provides status, personal identity, ego-strokes, a sense of belonging to a very special, highly articulate, ever-so-clever sisterhood. Knowledge provides entrance to many spheres beyond the university; and it confers on an initiate the right to monitor the gates, to determine who else gets in – and, even more, who else gets through the very bottom layers and thus gains entry to the world of "liberal" (non-manual) jobs in the information society.

When such power exists at the group, institutional, or individual level, there are bound to be struggles over it. Universities often speak of themselves in mythological terms as communities of scholars, disinterested pursuers of truth, disseminators of knowledge, transcribers of culture – all of which is true to a degree but is not the whole truth. The whole truth would have to include the interminable conflicts over administrative decisions, petty wars over control of either spatial or ideological territory, what he said to her and vice versa. It would also have to include the insufferable self-righteousness whenever the conflict over power takes on the appearance of conflict over ideas or moral codes. This is what the political science affair was, a conflict over power with the appearance of something more elevated.

The traditionalists stumble on, believing that these assaults are at the margins, that the university is still dedicated to the search for truth and beauty. Their ignorance of the implications of the changes surrounding them is one reason why the assaults are successful. Yes, they believe in inclusiveness and are quite happy to increase the proportion of women (or members of ethnic minorities, or Aboriginal people, or persons with different sexual orientations, or handicapped people) in their ranks if sufficient funds for recruitment are available. They truly feel no threat from inclusiveness. But they do not consider that this inclusiveness impinges in any way on the curriculum, on decisions about standards, on funding and research activity, or on the mission of the university. They have not made a choice between truth and advocacy because the choice has never been put to them in that way, and they have not chosen inclusiveness over meritocracy for the same reason.

Yet the issues surrounding them do impinge on the curriculum and on decisions about their work and the university's mission. They might first notice this when they want to recruit a standard variety of scholar and are suddenly caught in a political battle against an organized coalition of groups who want someone else in the job; or when a favourite is being wooed by other universities and the coalition demands that the salary and perks be immensely increased in order to keep their candidate. This used to happen when diverse "old boys" networks contested power; now the struggle is to ensure that no new boys join the club. And administrators regularly give in because a political battle on grounds that are claimed to be "sexism and racism" is too costly.

Framed as practical questions, further issues might be: Should those who control women's studies and gender research centres have more power over the total curriculum than the discipline-based departments? What should be the relative powers of institutes for sustainable development research and centres for entrepreneurship vis-a-vis departments of archaeology and mineral engineering? Should recruitment searches for academic departments be vetted by equity officers? Should representatives of women's groups or of diverse ethnic groups have veto powers over academic appointments? And how much of the university's resources should be spent on sexual harassment investigations or student counselling services compared with that spent on French literature or second-year biology? These are all immediate issues on most campuses across North America.

Once the challenge is mounted on one front, it is only a matter of time before it appears across the spectrum wherever power is played out: in the learned journals, the professional associations, and the various offices of the university and other institutions. If new players can capture these other theatres, they become ascendant in the university because they gain control of the curriculum, the channels for promotion and tenure, and the recruitment and retention of faculty. Power in the university is the same as power anywhere, and it is not to be treated lightly.

Other organizations attached to academe are also involved in the struggle for power. What are the relative powers of the Royal Society

of Canada, the Society for Academic Freedom and Scholarship, the
Alliance of Female Academics across Campuses, the Academic
Women's Association, the Civil Liberties Association, and numerous
professional associations and unions of university teachers? And what
are the relative powers of a dean of this or a dean of that, a vice-
president, and a student senator? Line officers in the university are
often outflanked by the spokespersons for social movements, and many
administrators in North American universities would vastly prefer to
have campus peace (or perhaps be portrayed as a moral leader on
behalf of women and minorities) than to take a strong stand for the
rational tradition in universities. Power is never stable, but when a
university is unsure of its bearings and unclear about its central
mission, the scramble for power permeates all else on the campus.

ACADEMIC FREEDOM

In times past, scholars mounted resistance to business and political
groups that tried to muzzle them when they talked about class and
economic power or corruption in politics. Occasionally a religious
institution became the opponent of secular intellectuals. Academic
freedom was the battle-cry for the campus, and enlightened politi-
cians, university administrators, and business leaders ultimately
backed up the academics. It was understood by the more enlightened
leaders of society that academics had to be allowed to speak freely
and to suffer no job loss when they made observations that discom-
fited the population.

Although enlightenment and academic freedom were joined in the
recent past, a curious revision of both terms has taken place in
universities today. Those who defend academic freedom find themselves in conflict with an entirely different set of opponents: feminists,
representatives of diverse ethnic groups, and various minority-group
organizations. In times past, the freedom fighters would have been in
alliance with these groups, defending their right to equal treatment.
But no longer are these groups demanding equal treatment, and they
need no defenders. They are engaged in a power struggle with the very
folk who used to defend them. The struggle is played out as morality
theatre. The competing groups argue that many things should not be
said in classrooms or elsewhere on campus, that many forms of
behaviour should not be tolerated, that some subjects should not be
taught, and that other subjects must be added. The traditional political
positions of left and right are washed out in these battles, and people
on both sides find themselves aligned with otherwise incompatible
allies.

Academic freedom is not at issue in the level of behaviour that involves hugging, dating, smirking, and crude sexist comments: this type of behaviour cannot be defended on the grounds of academic freedom, and universities have reasonable grounds (the legal grounds that exist beyond their gates, actually) for penalizing employees who engage in such behaviour. But defending a research project that explores the genetic bases for different behaviour of women and men, or expressing a negative assessment of feminist theory, may be much more controversial. These kinds of activity may be defensible under the old rules for academic freedom, but the new morality might define them as unacceptable and incorrect.

This puts academics of the old school in a tough spot. Thinking of themselves as liberal and left-liberal scholars, they now find themselves allied with spokespersons who represent conservative or even right-conservative politics. They may reject the term "political correctness" and yet find themselves in a hostile relationship with others precisely on the grounds of what is correct speech or proper behaviour. The dilemma here is that no one is obviously wrong in these struggles. Those who defend the new morality speak about inclusiveness, making everyone welcome, preventing the dissemination of hate literature or mean and discriminatory words. They remind one another of the worst parts of human history and blame universities for their contribution to evil civilizations of the past. Those who defend academic freedom speak of tolerance for diversity, equality of opportunity, and meritoriousness, and defend the liberal tradition of freedom. Both sides tend to be self-righteous because both are convinced that they represent the moral highroad; and although they are in head-on conflict, they both do.

When the moral highroads are brought down to earth in a particular case, however, they tend to disintegrate. The case in point included both dumb and mundane comments from faculty which were elevated by the complainants and McEwen to the level of sexist or racist observations. That "blacks were at the bottom of the hierarchy in South Africa," for example, seemed an unlikely statement to require an academic freedom defence. The "gentlemen prefer blondes" statement required a kick in the pants for an outdated professor, but it was hardly worth the label "sexist." The fact that these incidents were scarcely worthy of attack or defence by either group of moral high-grounders signifies that this fight – like many others across North American campuses – was not about the actual content of the case. In part, it was about whether universities will continue to set so much of the cultural agenda for these societies, and academic freedom is an incidental loss along the way.

MERITOCRACY AND SERVICE

The power of the meritocracy would be less offensive if the society were persuaded that it operated in the interests of society at large. Science and the scientific method were viewed as the carriers of progress, peace, and prosperity for the better part of the last three centuries.The capacity of humans to control nature, which is what science was all about, gave rise to the industrial society in all its manifestations, from indoor plumbing to rapid air travel. Its benefits notwithstanding, for some people science is linked to ecological damage caused by industrial processes and to the subordination of people to machines. Science, at the end of the twentieth century, is no longer taken for granted as a positive benefit to humankind.

Science that conquered other parts of the natural world was one thing, but science that examines and potentially conquers human nature is another and even more frightening undertaking, from some perspectives. Such an examination might include, for example, the genetic bases for sexual orientation and for differences of various kinds between men and women. Scientists who study race and class or race and intelligence also claim to use the scientific method, though the rest of the scientific world has disowned those who claim to have found a racial basis to intelligence. In part, this is because the definitions of race are so problematic and are sometimes reliant on little more than skin colour. The point is that the scientific method is neutral with reference to human values: it can be used to investigate virtually any subject. It can be used to improve living conditions for people or to harm people; it can make people feel good or make them uncomfortable.

Science might make people feel uncomfortable because it tries to tell truths. While universities have always prided themselves (whether rightly or not) as progressive institutions that advocate good social policy, the advocacy in the past was linked, at least ideologically, to the pursuit of truth. When the two are divorced, advocacy loses its legitimate base. In the social sciences and humanities, there are faculty and students who feel that the divorce is inevitable; that the entire point of the university now is to reinvent the world. If one looks at the criticism of curriculum and faculty throughout the Report, one gains glimpses of what the utopian world would look like: no hierarchy, no patriarchy, no authority, inclusion of everyone equally, and dissolution of the Western canon. If Shakespeare is nothing more than a dead white European male and Rousseau is not worth reading because he abandoned his own children, one might ask, Why should we maintain the liberal arts at expensive universities? To do away with these subjects would be a cheap solution to the very substantial dilemma the society faces as costs of higher education exceed capacity. To insist that there are differences, that some things have quality beyond others, is to join the Western tradition (even if the canon in question is not of Western origin), and this is inconsistent with the critique.

The curious thing about popular postmodernism is that despite its nihilistic message, it is used for purposes of moral transformation. Nothing matters – yet it is vitally important that no one should use swearwords or utter a discriminatory phrase in the classroom. Students should be comfortable at all times; no one should ever feel excluded from the academy. What is then actually being said is that academic standards associated with meritocracy are no longer valid; moral standards associated with inclusiveness are to take their place.

TRUTH VS INCLUSIVENESS

The political science affair was symptomatic of the intellectual as well as moral dilemmas of contemporary universities. It revealed a core problem – that universities are no longer sure what they are about and can no longer defend with assurance the Western tradition of scholarship.[3] The fact that credentialled and respected academic leaders accepted the Report and the general condemnation of "white" men is a testament to the paucity of conviction about the value of what Searle called the Western rational tradition.

Is this a loss of faith (if one dare use such a term in reference to a rational tradition) in Western society? Is it a loss of faith in the intellectual inquiry within that tradition? It may be both. At the most dramatic, one might argue that Western society is turning away from its cultural inheritance. Perhaps as the end of European/American hegemony comes into view, with the inevitability of dramatic cultural change upon us, we shun the culture that nurtured us – shamed somehow and willing to let it be defamed as well as transformed, and no longer willing to defend its intellectual tradition. Rather than seeing its virtues, we note its evils: patriarchy, capitalism, imperialism, ecological damage ... The list is long, alas, and the condemnations are often justified.

A less dramatic view might be that the mass-production machine had turned out a generation of teachers and administrators who themselves were unfamiliar with the tradition. They had perhaps lost the sense of scholarly mission and become technocrats and careerists in the public bureaucracy. In the mills that universities had become, maybe there was no time and space for graduate students to consider the diverse and conflicting views of the philosophers of science and education. Possibly, graduates moved into narrow specialized slots at universities, taught their narrowly defined subjects, did their narrowly identified research, and never really had to decide what the whole enterprise was about. The modern university may have done a complete turnaround and rejected all that Cardinal Newman hoped for it; indeed, inadvertently and in simple ignorance, it may have turned off the light that made the enterprise worthwhile.

The natural and applied sciences have always been embedded in the rationalist tradition, and they could point to stunning theoretical and technological outcomes from that approach. Heisenberg's uncertainty principle and other caveats notwithstanding, the results of science included the conviction that some things were known, that more would be known, and that the method for seeking knowledge worked. The humanities and social sciences never did attain this degree of certainty and never could point to concrete and unambiguous results of their work. The attack on the rationalist tradition is, not surprisingly, centred in the liberal arts rather than in the natural and applied sciences.

The attack is particularly strong in those fields where external events have made a mockery of much of the literature, and political science may be one of these, though not the only one. Pax Americana has faded, and a discipline that emerged within it and the American hegemonic version of international relations and domestic politics could be in trouble. While continuing to teach the curriculum of a fading world power, some of its practitioners are not ready for the rivalry of other, now powerful, perspectives on their subject. Some observers thought that the flare-ups in three Canadian political science departments were related to the discipline's concern with power; perhaps they were, but perhaps they were as much the result of a failure to understand it.

Neo-Marxism is viewed as an alternative less because the proponents have read Marx than because American political science never took Marx seriously. But Marxism, from the perspective of the complainants, has three serious defects at this stage: it is as embedded in the Western rationalist tradition as what it might supplant; it concentrates on class, virtually ignoring gender and ethnicity; and it is ineluctably tied to historical materialism in the midst of the much-touted information revolution. Feminist theory obviously does provide new insights and a very different perspective on the nature of power. Postmodernism allows the protagonists to take off their gloves and to abandon the search for truth in favour of a social movement. From Marx, postmodernism took the lesson that the point of philosophy is to transform, not merely understand, the world.

CLASS STRUGGLE VS SEXISM, RACISM

The Western world has encountered revolutionary movements in the past, but these have generally come in the form of class struggles. It was notable that in neither the affair at UBC nor in others like it across North America did the rhetoric of class struggle emerge. In the 1990s, the unequal distribution of power was expressed in terms of sexism and racism; it was not a ruling class that now had power, not an elite, not the bourgeoisie, the corporate directors, the board of governors, or any other of the traditional groups identified as power holders. It was "white" men, all "white" men, and their opponents were women and all "persons of colour." Yet the struggle was not really about sexism and racism *per se*; and that is why it did not matter whether the particular men in a particular department were actually guilty as charged. What mattered was that all men throughout the university were guilty of a higher charge: the possession of power.

While we must consider the amount of knowledge and power inherent in universities, we should not lose sight of the displaced class dimension. All this is happening in a world in which the rich are getting richer and, as statistics in every industrial country are now showing, the poor are getting poorer and there are ever more of them. The middle class is diminishing in size and in power, and it was this great middle class that sustained the democratic universities of the postwar period. In recent years, students have chosen to see their dilemmas in terms of gender, race or ethnicity, and sexual orientation, and university administrators and tenured faculty have encouraged them in this approach. No one has been speaking of classes, no one has been questioning the distribution of income that would eventually and fundamentally alter the opportunities to attend university. And because they were so determined to label their problems sexism and racism, students failed to find allies in a general population outside the gates whose issues are poverty, unemployment, and class inequalities. Although sexism and racism also are issues beyond the gates, especially in knowledge-based centres such as the media industry, a large part of the population has other and even more pressing issues to cope with.

SUBSTANCE AND PROCESS

If agreement is the final arbiter of ideas, and if a consensus were to be reached that a department was guilty of various crimes labelled sexism and racism, would that constitute sufficient proof of its guilt? The answer is no longer obvious, because the gulf between rationalism and postmodernism blurs the meaning of all the essential terms.

There can be little doubt that the allegations about hugging, asking for dates, and the like, if true, constituted a rather crude form of sexism – not so much overtly harmful as disrespectful of female students. Proponents on both sides of the great debate might agree that these acts were sexist; indeed, most colleagues in the beleaguered Department of Political Science accepted that. For the rationalist, what mattered was that there was no evidence of discrimination at the level of grades and awards and that the alleged withdrawals did not occur. There was no evidence that a change in curriculum was required to eliminate the "hugging" forms of sexism or that the curriculum was, in and of itself, sexist. Rorty and his colleagues would likely have used the same criteria for determining guilt, but obviously Ms McEwen and many who supported her position had different criteria. Given the different and unpredictable criteria, the entire episode became an exercise in realpolitik; as such, it was a struggle for public support rather than a struggle to determine the truth.

The search for truth with reference to allegations of this kind would necessarily take the form of a procedure generally called natural justice or due process, whereby the accused know of what and by whom they are accused, are provided with evidence and argument by their accuser, and are given a reasonable opportunity to present a defence. The accused remain innocent pending a guilty judgment based on the evidence and on a full and respectful hearing of both sides of the dispute. All of this is part and parcel of the same Western rationalistic tradition that stood behind universities for the past several centuries. Like the notion of distinterested scholarly investigation, it is part of the framework that enables a society to avoid arbitrary rule by persons and to ensure that evidence takes precedence over prejudice.

To argue, as some did when the flaws of the McEwen Report became widely recognized, that the fault lay with the terms of reference is not sufficient reason for ignoring the matter of due process. Let us suppose that the terms were the first of many flaws. The end result in that event (as would be the case if the terms were not at fault) would still be a report so seriously unjust that no action should have been taken on it. The appropriate response would have been to treat the McEwen Report as a preliminary input (and an expensive lesson to us all), and to set up a committee to determine how best to proceed with an internal inquiry into the more serious of the allegations.

One individual informed me that the concept of natural justice was a Western and Eurocentric one, and that my devotion to it suggested that I was racist. I reject this argument with some contempt, but in view of it I shall impose my personal view on the readers! I would argue that all cultures, great and small, have rules and laws, and that while these differ they may all lead to justice. The invocation of relativity does not justify treating the laws of any particular culture as being of no consequence while one is living in that culture and working in its institutions; certainly, it does not justify a claim of racism with respect to those who obey that culture's laws. We have a culture that originated in Europe, and we inherited and continued to develop its rules and laws. There is nothing shameful or racist about that, and to the extent that the rules and laws are fair and equitable, the body of law we have in Canada is a source of peace and civil relations amongst us. Regardless of its source, it is a major institution for the good in this society, and we, its beneficiaries, should vigilantly nurture it. To the extent that the laws are unfair or inequitable, we should be actively debating them and urging their reformulation. Such a stance would be far from destroying the law even if the needed reforms were extensive.

I think it especially important that universities cherish and defend the rule of law. Without it they would not exist; neither would the conditions in society that promote their development. In societies where the rule of law has never taken root or has disintegrated, universities have been closed and faculty have often been the first target of totalitarian regimes.

Sometimes people understand grand principles in the abstract but cannot apply them to the daily circumstances of their lives. Thus it is with the concept of natural justice, or due process. Sometimes the problem lies in the ordering of priorities. For some people in this case, due process took second place to their desire to cure sexism and racism. Perhaps they believed that the department was guilty as charged irre-spective of the flawed McEwen Report. If so, I suggest that they trivialized the issues of sexism and racism. We no longer lynch sus-pected murderers, we try them in a court of law. We no longer burn witches; we try to determine what if any laws they have violated. Similarly, we should not assume that because people have been accused of sexism and racism they are automatically guilty. These are not trivial charges, and the accused and accusers are in need of serious attention.

The comment about relative notions of law indicates a confusion about respect for diverse cultures within any one culture. Canada has tried to welcome people of all cultural origins and to allow them to retain their distinctive ethnic roots. The alternative – which was rejected – would have been integration into the primarily Anglo-Saxon culture of anglophone Canada or the francophone culture of Quebec. The Canadian way is a noble though inherently high-risk human experiment. Its chief critics are immigrants, who point out that there have to be limits to diversity if a nation is to be sustained; as well, that some cultural customs (for example, the circumcision of female infants, violent vendettas between families, the carrying of guns) are inconsistent with Canadian law and are wildly inconsistent with the relatively peaceful culture already established throughout the country. These critics are not arguing for homogeneity; what they support is a clear enunciation of where the limits are, for there are some features of Canadian culture that should not be ignored or negotiated out of existence.

Neil Bissoondath, an Indian immigrant from Trinidad and one of Canada's major writers, notes: "If Canada, as an historical, social, legal and cultural concept, does not demand respect for itself and its ideals, why should any respect be expected?"[4] Immigrants come to Canada precisely because it offers a relatively tolerant and humane environment, and Bissoondath argues that a failure to defend what is good in Canada is not the way to avoid racism and bigotry. On the contrary, Canadians can best defend diversity of ethnic origins by insisting on the retention of and respect for those features of Canadian culture that maintain tolerance, civility, and peace. Of these, due process and the rule of law are essential.

To insist on the rule of law in no way provides a rationale for racism. What it does is set out clear procedures for how we deal with racism once racism has been both defined and alleged to exist. If racism is defined in a way that includes any failure to appreciate subtle differences in culture or to accord all cultures absolute equality regardless of context and circumstance, then we are all racist because it is impossible for a human being to be totally aware and always conscious of subtle differences – or, in the conduct of normal classroom business, to accord all differences equal attention.

In some cultures men are invariably more important than women; a teacher in a Canadian university could not respect that custom except by ignoring Canadian culture's emphasis on gender equality. In some cultures a student must always bow to a professor and never argue – impossible habits and customs in a Canadian context, and consequently Canadian professors have to give such students gentle encouragement to think for themselves and reduce their deferential behaviour. Again, gift giving to professors is essential in some of the cultures from which students come to Canada, but this practice is inappropriate in Canada; so, again, professors are obliged to encourage students to adopt some features of the Canadian culture in order to survive and flourish in it. These are not racist acts on the part of the teacher; they are acts consistent with membership in a definite culture – that of Canada. There is nothing shameful about insisting on some limits to diversity in order to maintain the larger but still heterogeneous and tolerant society.

To allege racism in a heterogeneous society and in an extremely heterogeneous university context is a very serious matter. The B.C. Civil Liberties Association concluded that no evidence of racism was given in the McEwen Report, and it dismissed this charge with regard to the Department of Political Science. For the most part, I agree with this conclusion, though I think that the matter will not disappear so easily. Those who believe that every instance of insisting on some observance of Canadian law and custom is by its nature racist, or who are convinced that anything said and done by "white" Canadians is by its nature racist and defensive of privilege, will never agree that the behaviour complained about in the political science affair was not racist behaviour – whatever else it may have been.

If the faculty had listened to the unsaid words, if the students who complained had spoken to the accused instead of to external authorities, would this whole affair have been easily resolved? In connection with the pending human rights cases, McEwen stated, "In my judgment, all that is needed is for the respondents to simply 'listen' to what complainants are saying, to consider whether there are ways of being supportive of their concerns ... I am confident that, if a meaningful dialogue can take place in an atmosphere of mutual trust, then the subject complaints are readily amenable to informal resolution" (130). This is good advice to all university departments. Had she omitted all the rhetoric about "white" males, this message might well have reached its targets; instead, it was buried under the debris.

I doubt that such easy solutions were ever at hand. Whether the fault lay more with deaf faculty or self-pitying students I do not know, but I seriously doubt that the two were ever on the same wavelength for long enough to talk it out. And once it became a public affair, it grew well beyond the actual complaints. The spectators projected onto this stage their personal experiences of sexism suffered elsewhere, the racism of society more generally, and personal slights from other times and places. They imagined much that was not in the Report and magnified what was there – in thrall to a belief, rather than to evidence, that a group defined in a pejorative way as "white men" was guilty.

The political science affair involved a lot of stone throwing (as phrased by Helen Garner in a superb exploration of allegations of sexual misconduct at an Australian university).[5] I find myself wondering how far any privileged group (men, persons of a dominant ethnic group, administrators, and so on) should go in defining the light for those whom they propose to shepherd. I consider that much of the paternalism of well-intentioned men towards women whom they define as weak and in need of protection is arrogant and insulting (the same men often shrink from contact with strong independent women);

similarly insulting is much of the breast beating of "white" privileged men. I personally find the voluntary assumption of victimhood pathetic. And, finally, I wonder what it is in the human psyche that urges us to define sin in accordance with our prejudices and to label others whom we do not like as sinners.

On the other hand, I wondered about the self-serving arguments for academic freedom. I favour freedom of speech, academic or otherwise – and actually I think that non-academics are more in need of protection than my colleagues – but the limits to free speech are in need of defence too. Faculty members sometimes use their positions as pulpits, preaching their particular brand of politics, religion, philosophy, or gossip. I have done this myself in times past, and I know too well how easily one slips into it and how few restraints there are.

The freedom is rooted in the notion that faculty are seeking truth and that they are, both by temperament and training, philosophically disposed towards balance and fairness. It is rather a lot to assume, especially in the mass-education systems that universities have become. If society at large is, as claimed, sexist and racist, it follows that some professors will be of the same persuasions. Should they have the freedom to speak their views in a classroom in which they also have the power to evaluate students? Alternatively, if professors see their task as bringing about large-scale social change and if they have no commitment to the notion of truth, should they have the freedom to use the classroom as a propaganda dissemination centre? Universities have not even tried to come to grips with these issues, and the notion of academic freedom has fallen into disrepute because too often its limits have been ignored.

TRUTH AND BIOGRAPHY

Those who defend the pursuit of truth and objective scholarship – of whom I am unabashedly one – are obliged to acknowledge some fundamental truths in the arguments of those who argue that all intellectual positions are influenced (I shall not go so far as to say determined) by biographical circumstances. There is little doubt, for a relevant example, that men have defined much of the literary and social science canon; that women might well have defined it otherwise, have measured it in different ways, have prized some ideas not understood by powerful men, or have ignored some that appealed to them. That ascribed characteristics have affected opportunities in academia as elsewhere is surely true, by systemic even if not intentional means.

Can one, then, continue to hold the view that these disciplines should/can seek truth, that objective scholarship is possible? Because the subject matter is humanity and culture, the task is exceptionally difficult. Yet I take the position that a platonic image of truth is still to be preferred to a slippery version of relativity. Human brains may never achieve sufficient insight to escape the biases of gender, ethnicity, class, religion, and fashion, but it is worth trying to do so. To move beyond *ad hominem* or *ad feminam* arguments and advance towards a genuine appreciation of alternative understandings and diverse principles is an objective of the humanities and social sciences. It is a worthwhile objective but insufficient in itself. Sometimes we can go beyond this, to weigh diverse principles in the light of all the information and knowledge we can bring to the study. We do this when we imagine a truth "out there" and strive to discover it anew with each issue. Even when the most one can ever hope for is to disprove some arguments – that is, to show that truth does not lie in them – that is an advance in our understanding.

How can we square such a notion with the evident reality of disciplines that shift with empires and are subject to ideological fads and fashions? All the social sciences have substantial ideological components. Interestingly – and significantly – the biases differ between allied subjects. One is more likely to be exposed to neo-Marxism, postmodernism, or feminism in human geography or sociology than in mainstream political science, but this does not make these other subjects less biased. What occurs here is that a perspective is developed as far as it can go within a discipline; those who choose to study in this discipline pursue that line until it exhausts itself. At that point the discipline either renews itself, borrowing from neighbouring disciplines and re-examining its basic premises, or it gradually disappears from the curriculum. Knowledge does accumulate at an exceedingly slow pace as competing paradigms seek their respective truths. This interpretation is consistent with Kuhn's arguments on the development of science, but it insists on the external reality of the subject under investigation and on the possibility of approaching that. Both that which is socially constructed and the world beyond social construction are objective realities independent of our capacity to comprehend them.

When all is said and done, what is the role of the university at the conclusion of the twentieth century? After this exploration of the issues, I end up still believing that a scholarly society should strive to create equitable processes but that it must not abandon tolerance (as in agreeing to a zero degree of it), natural justice, or notions of reform in favour of a revolution with as yet unstated intentions. And I still think it not a bad objective to seek a fair representation of truth. But I must confess to a substantial increase in scepticism about the university's capacity to be both the moral leader and the intellectual storehouse for society. Morality is many sided, and while sexism as it was alleged in this case may be repugnant, it is equally repugnant to impose narrow language codes on others and to call them names based on their skin colour.

One returns to the Victorians: a university should strive to inculcate philosophical habits of mind and an appreciation for both goodness and knowledge, a desire for wisdom. But ultimately there is only one distinguishing feature of a university compared with any other institution. Its mandate is to seek truth. Without this, there is no need for or unique meaning to such an institution.

Notes

CHAPTER ONE

1 One vice-president got carried away on a radio show when noting the difference between a trivial and a serious complaint. For an example of the trivial, she cited an instance described in the investigator's report. For an example of the serious, she cited exchange of grades for sexual favours. As two graduate students pointed out, nowhere in all the reams of accusations against faculty in political science was any such charge ever made. The vice-president graciously apologized.

2 University of British Columbia Equity Office, *Discrimination and Harassment, Clarifying the Nature of Complaints and their Resolution* (Vancouver: UBC, 1996), 1–3.

3 Philip Resnick had spoken in defence of these core values at a faculty meeting. His comments were published in the *Globe and Mail*, 10 September 1995.

4 Marjorie Griffin Cohen, Gillian Creese, and Veronica Strong-Boag, "The Campus Struggle for Pluralism, Tolerance, Mutual Respect," *Vancouver Sun*, 5 October 1995.

5 The label "Red Guards" and implications of parallels were printed in *B.C. Report*, September 1995.

6 As reported in the *Globe and Mail*, 7 September 1995.

CHAPTER TWO

1 John R. Searle, "Rationality and Realism: What is at Stake?" *Daedalus* 122, no. 4 (Fall 1992): 69. The quotation is from *Speaking for the Humanities* (ACLS Occasional Paper no. 7, 1989), 18.

2 The term "postmodernism" was initially used in architecture in the late 1940s, and later it was formulated as a cultural theory in the works of

Jacques Derrida, Roland Barthes, Jacques Lacan, Michel Foucault, and Jean-François Lyotard. Derrida is credited with the extension of post-modernist ideas under the rubric of deconstructionism.

3 T.S. Kuhn, *The Structure of Scientific Revolutions* (Chicago: University of Chicago Press, 1962). See also T.S. Kuhn, "Afterwords," in *World Changes: Thomas Kuhn and the Nature of Science*, ed. Paul Horwich (Cambridge, Mass.: MIT Press, 1993).

4 Richard Rorty, draft of lecture "Does Academic Freedom Have Philosophical Presuppositions?" as presented at UBC in 1994. The drafts of several lectures were made available on condition that they not be quoted directly because they were not yet published.

5 Searle, "Rationality and Realism," 70–1.

6 Kate Millett, *Sexual Politics* (New York: Avon, 1970).

7 Veronica Strong-Boag, director, Centre for Research in Women's Studies and Gender Relations, "Privilege and Responsibility: Hard Questions about Academic Freedom" (address to UBC Faculty Association, November 1995), abbreviated version published in *Newsletter 6*, no. 1 (Winter 1996).

8 Christina Hoff Sommers, *Who Stole Feminism? How Women Have Betrayed Women* (New York: Simon and Schuster, 1994), 21.

9 Rene Denfeld, *The New Victorians* (New York: Warner Books, 1996).

10 First published in 1852, this is available under the title *Essays on University Subjects* (London: Everyman's Library). The selections here are from excerpts in *The College Survey of English Literature* (New York: Harcourt, Brace, 1950), 881–8.

11 Matthew Arnold, *Culture and Anarchy* (1869; rev. edn., ed. J. Dover Wilson, Cambridge: Cambridge University Press, 1969). The selections quoted here are from chap. 1.

12 Philip Resnick, "In Defence of the Liberal University," UBC *Alumni Chronicle*, Spring 1996, 18–19.

13 The two cultures were examined most intensively by C.P. Snow in a series of novels about British universities, published in the 1930s to 1950s.

14 *Training for What?* (Victoria: B.C. Labour Force Development Board, 1995).

CHAPTER THREE

1 The dean of the Faculty of Graduate Studies (FOGS) has authority over graduate programs and may close a graduate program or suspend admissions for cause. Faculty members, however, are under the jurisdiction of the general faculties, in this case the Faculty of Arts.

2 The external review, in which this is also stated, was not then public, so either the students and the external reviewer had coincidentally arrived at the same conclusion or one of them had influenced the other through exchanges not included in the written submission.

3 A lecturer without long-term tenure, hired from year to year. The normal length of stay at one university is from two to three years.

CHAPTER FOUR

1 Compared with most other departments in the Faculty of Arts, the Department of Political Science was extremely fortunate; the others lost faculty members rather than gaining them. The gains reflected in part the establishment of major Asian research centres that cross-appointed faculty, of whom two were in political science.

2 Full-time equivalent (FTE) is a standardized measure taking head-counts multiplied by course credit values in all courses divided by a standard 30-credit-hour load.

3 These data are taken from departmental compilations. There is always some flux in student data as individuals come into and leave programs, so any compilation might change by one or two individuals over the period of a few months.

4 Identification of past students was tentative; they were not self-identified.

5 These lists included a number of students who did not turn up or who withdrew within a few weeks and were not included in the withdrawal data cited earlier. After noting that the numbers were equal for men and women, I excluded them from further consideration. Other nonacademic reasons included lack of funds (one male), winning a fellowship to another university (one male), and death (one female).

6 Neil Guppy, covering letter to Joan McEwen with summary results for selected questions, copied to me and others on 17 December 1994. These data have since been made available to others and are now in the public realm.

7 Neil Guppy and Marsha Trew, "Graduate Student Experience at UBC: An Assessment. Final Report," September 1995, 23–4.

8 Reports after 1994 could not receive this guarantee because of the provincial government's "freedom of information" legislation.

CHAPTER FIVE

1 John G. Grace, "Suspension of Graduate Admissions in Department of Political Science," communication to the Graduate Council, 10 October 1995.

2 Page numbers in brackets following quotations or summaries refer to the *Report in Respect of the Political Science Department of the University of British Columbia*, prepared by Joan McEwen, 15 June 1995.

3 See below regarding the comments on this in the *Advocate*.

4 I asked Dr Sharon Kahn, UBC's associate vice-president, equity, to provide me with some working definitions for "sexism," "racism," "systemic," and "pervasive," rather than relying on formal dictionary definitions. My usage has been close to her suggestions. The definitions of sexism and racism given in chapter 1 are abbreviated but are consistent with these.

5 *Oxford Illustrated Dictionary* (Oxford: Clarendon Press, 1962).

6 This is from a widely distributed letter addressed to Dr Strangway, president of UBC, dated 13 July 1995.

7 "Entre Nous," *Advocate* 53, no. 5 (September 1995).

8 Doug Saunders, "Report 'Flawed,' UBC Arts Dean Says," *Globe and Mail*, 15 July 1995.

9 Lesley Krueger, "A Few Are Influencing a Lot at UBC," *Globe and Mail*, 6 October 1995.

10 This individual gave permission to print this section from a letter dated 14 July 1995.

11 This individual and others who wrote to the president identified themselves in their letters (which were widely distributed), but except where I have quoted directly and received permission from the authors to do so, I have not used names in this text.

12 R. Kenneth Carty, Robert H. Jackson, Paul Marantz, and Diane K. Mauzy, letter dated 2 June 1995.

CHAPTER SIX

1 This is inevitable in just about any department, because a supervisor cannot take on a student whose theoretical or empirical interests are outside her/his own field of expertise. This may be a serious flaw in the way graduate education is carried on, but it is not peculiar to this department.

2 Ms McEwen listed each item separately, though from the context here or elsewhere in her report it seems that the same student was making a protracted complaint against the same male white professor in the first two items on this list. The investigator used terms such as "more than one student" or "many female students," so the reader cannot judge whether the behaviour (if it occurred as alleged) was a regular feature of the department exhibited by all or most professors, or a particular incident involving one professor and one student complainant.

3 The section on student evaluations opened with this disclaimer: "While no allegations of racism or sexism were made in respect of grading in general, numerous instances were cited of discriminatory grading and evaluation practices by various professors." The instances cited have all the appearances of allegations, and there is no obvious reason for the disclaimer.

4 The contradiction between these two items is not noted by McEwen.

5 The investigation occurred in 1994–95; the minutes cited date to March 1991.

6 The term "black" is in the text, though the same student appears to be called "of colour" elsewhere.

7 The nature of the facial language is not clear in the text, i.e., whether it was "leering," "dismissive," or otherwise.

8 From the text it appears that this was the same student whose person brought about the facial expressions noted in the previous complaint. It is not explained how the student would know what occurred at the meeting since awards meetings are not open to students.

9 This was in reference to the Keate case, which I discussed in chapter 3. It was described at length elsewhere in the Report.

10 McEwen's numbers on p. 105 differ from university records.

CHAPTER SEVEN

1 Karen Gram, "Report Blasts UBC for Discrimination," *Vancouver Sun*, 22 June 1995.

2 These are contained in chapter 4 of the McEwen Report, mainly under the heading "Inappropriate Socializing and Sexual/Racial Harassment."

3 Nicole Parten, "Student Sought $40,000 to Drop Charges," *Vancouver Sun*, 24 June 1995.

4 *Globe and Mail*, 23 June 1995.

5 UBC faculty would likely be aware that the B.C. Privacy Act effectively prohibits the giving out of any names and addresses without written permission.

6 A letter writer to the *Globe and Mail* characterized this contribution from the vice-president, academic as akin to "the bird that flew in ever-diminishing circles until something very unpleasant happened" (11 July 1995).

7 This I discovered much later and by accident. I was told that the staff representative to the board had informed a union meeting that the dean of FoGS had come to the board meeting to present his views but that the dean of arts had not come (the clear implication being that she had refused or had been too arrogant to attend). I wrote immediately to the chairperson to request that the board be informed that I

was never invited and that had I been invited I would most certainly have turned up. The response was a surprised statement to the effect that the chair understood that I had been invited and that the board accepted my regrets in good faith (I have no idea who submitted my regrets!).

8 Public letter to Dr David Strangway, UBC president, from John Westwood, executive director, B.C. Civil Liberties Association, 13 July 1995.

9 *Ubyssey*, 20 July 1995.

10 Stephen Hume, "The Bias That Reduces a Colleague to an Obscenity," *Vancouver Sun*, 26 July 1995.

11 *Globe and Mail*, 6 September 1995.

12 "Shades of the Red Guards," *B.C. Report*, September 1995.

13 "Counterattack on a Witch Hunt," *B.C. Report*, September 1995.

14 The Department of Political Science, in fact, had gone into supplicant posture for most of the debate: it was incapable of orchestrating anything. If by "orchestration" is meant merely that there were critics, then of course the charge is true. I was a critic, so were the heads and directors of most departments in arts who signed a petition to remove the suspension, and five went further to demand a special meeting of the Faculty of Arts to debate the issues. To request a debate on a university campus is not the equivalent of orchestrating opposition.

15 But these various statements referred to a wide variety of problems, and were not admissions of sexist and racist practices. As well, the apparent consistency in noting problems is not surprising if the complainants in all cases were the same individuals.

16 See chapter 5 regarding the group, including the dean of FoGS, who had input into the terms of reference and the choice of Ms McEwen.

17 See chapter 5 for discussion on this point.

18 No other suspensions involved charges of racism and sexism; they may well have included academic issues.

19 The dean's memory fails him. Publicity was created by statements given by Ms Jones to the media (see chapter 3 for details). The press releases regarding the department's decision were prepared by the university media relations office in full consultation with the central administration and with the knowledge of the dean of FoGS. The decision to make the report public was in deference to the graduate students and the dean of FoGS's concern for them.

20 UBC *Alumni Chronicle*, Winter 1995, 16.

CHAPTER EIGHT

1 Kal Holsti, correspondence widely circulated.

CHAPTER NINE

1 A helpful analysis of this feature is given by Neil J. Smelser in "The Politics of Ambivalence: Diversity in the Research Universities," *Daedalus* 122, no. 4 (1993): 37–53.

2 David Mamet, *Oleanna* (New York: Vintage Books, 1992), presents the conflicts in his memorable play. This is used extensively to illustrate an essay on the subject by Jonathan R. Cole, "Balancing Acts: Dilemmas of Choice Facing Research Universities," in *Daedalus* 122, no. 4 (1993): 1–36.

3 For a thoughtful essay on this subject, see Louis Menand, "What Are Universities For?" *Harpers*, December 1991, 47–55.

4 Neil Bissoondath, *Selling Illusions: The Cult of Multiculturalism in Canada* (Toronto: Penguin, 1994). See also Richard Gwyn, *Nationalism without Walls: The Unbearable Lightness of Being Canadian* (Toronto: McClelland and Stewart, 1995).

5 Helen Garner, *The First Stone* (Picador: Sydney, 1995).